HAFED & HERMES

'Dead' for 2,000 years these two friends of Jesus reveal fascinating facts concerning Christ, the ancient world, and the world of spirit. Their revelations became a best-selling book *(Hafed, a Prince of Persia)* in Victorian Britain, and at the request of spirit, Ronald Wright has revised and abridged the original work for modern readers. Part One was published (Regency Press) in January, 1988 under its original title. This is Part Two.

D0529118

HAFED & HERMES

*

Edited and Abridged
by
Ronald Wright

REVELATION PRESS
5 MEAD LANE
HERTFORD SG13 7AG

Published by Revelation Press, 5 Mead Lane, Hertford SG13 7AG

ISBN 0 9514038 1 8

Printed in England by Booksprint, Bristol

INTRODUCTION

As most readers are probably aware, this volume forms part of a series of spirit communications which Hafed and Hermes passed on to a group of Scottish researchers investigating psychic phenomena between the years of 1869 and 1873. During that time one hundred seances were held in the presence of Mr David Duguid, a Glasgow medium of considerable repute, and notes being taken on each occasion, these were published in the form of a best-selling book in 1875.

What made these communications so important was the fact that one of the spirits claimed to be one of the three Magi of biblical fame, whilst the other stated that he had been a childhood friend of Jesus in Egypt, and a disciple later in Israel.

However despite the book's original popularity, Victorian and Edwardian Britain was at that time so strongly in the grip of religious orthodoxy, that virtually all copies of the book were to disappear during the next century. Indeed one man has testified that he spent *forty years* trying to locate a copy, even enlisting the services of a 'world search' organisation, all without success. All of which only goes to highlight my own extraordinary rediscovery of the book—through spirit guidance, and my efforts to revive the contents at their request.

It all began one day when a spirit voice spoke to me and declared that I was to 'help' in the writing of a 'most important book'—at that time I was completely unaware of the existence of either Hafed or his book.

I was told that I would encounter 'Three men all dressed in black who shall lead you to the next stage of your spiritual adventure.' Sure enough some months later I *did* meet these men in the Church of St. Bartholomew the Great, at Smithfield, and was told by one of them that I should try to locate a copy of the 'Hafed' book, although I was warned that it might take many months or even years to do so.

Astonishingly when I commenced my search the following day, I was guided by spirit into a shop where a copy of the book had been sold to the proprietor only *minutes* before!

Having read the book I became aware that the original version was much too difficult for a modern public to appreciate, and so immediately set to work to revise and abridge the contents. I also decided to split the book into two parts, and the first portion, dealing with the earthly life of Hafed, was published in December, 1987, by Regency Press Ltd. The second, you now hold in your hands, and I hope it may afford you as much pleasure and enlightenment as it gave me when I first read the original.

I also pray that a new phase in the history of the world will shortly emerge when people shall once again communicate freely with the superior minds of spirit and thereby shed greater understanding and tolerance amongst all the peoples of the earth, spreading light and goodwill where at present there exists greed and selfishness, spiritual understanding and harmony where there is now ignorance and destructive materialism. The Golden Age *can* become a reality, but only when people replace their self-interest and their nationalism with a true concern for others first and foremost.

Follow the pathway of light that even now unfurls before you, and rich shall be your rewards.

Ronald Wright

CONTENTS

Hafed speaks of life in spirit

Communications from Hermes

Questions Answered

HAFED

speaks of

life in the spirit

1

The great reunion

The leaving of the mortal body and the entrance into spirit-life may be said to be a new birth—a child from mother earth taking on immortality; and just as a child wakes up into consciousness of its surroundings in the earth-life, so many of those who pass away from earth awake in the spirit world; or, as the tiny insect which lies torpid during the long hours of winter, rises up into summer life in newness of form and faculty, and seeks its provender from flower to flower, so there are some who, freed from the material shell, rise up with newness of life and power into the celestial region of light and love and beauty.

I looked around me. It was a glorious change indeed, and one I had often longed for; for now I had joined those loved ones who had gone before.

First my beloved wife embraced me, and then my child, now a stately man, hung on my neck. I could hardly realise that which I saw. But as I looked I recognised my own dear father and mother. Then the whole region shook with a grand burst of harmonious music, while heavenly heralds proclaimed welcome to the martyrs for Jesus. I turned to one and inquired if such a welcome was accorded to every one.

'Yes,' he said, 'but you seem to have got a louder welcome.'

I could hardly keep from feeling that it was all a dream—a vision. But this could not be; for here I was, not alone, but united once more to those dear ones who had gone before, those whom I had loved on earth now surrounded me and conversed with me, and all were anxious to explain to me thousands of new subjects which met my view on every side.

My venerable friend, whom I had known on earth as the old Egyptian priest, Issha, came forward and invited me to go with him to the great temple. Our way to the temple was carpeted with the freshest verdure, while thousands of flowers of the loveliest hues and fragrance created within me a delight which mortal man cannot realise. My soul was ravished by the scene. 'And this is heaven!' I exclaimed. 'It is worth ten thousand lives on earth to live but one day here.'

At length the great temple burst into view. It was a glorious object, on which the eye might rest in ever-increasing admiration, with its great dome reaching far, far into space, while the rows of its massive transparent pillars stood out in unapproachable grandeur. I think there must have been a degree of earthliness still clinging to me, for I felt somewhat dazzled as the bright ones looked on me. But such sensations soon wore off, and earthly weaknesses were no longer felt.

On reaching the temple, I observed a vast body of horsemen drawn up; they were thousands in number, and panoplied in bright and glittering armour, and standing at their head I beheld him who had been my spirit guide on earth! He it was who appeared as the commander of the glorious host, amongst which I observed hundreds of those who had once been my fellow-warriors and fellow-labourers. Here they were again ready to do battle for truth and righteousness.

As I gazed in awe and wonder on the gloriously-clad throng, a shout as if from ten thousand trumpets rent the air, and such as I had never heard before. I turned to my Egyptian friend, and asked him what it meant, remarking, 'The throats from which such sounds proceed must surely be made of silver, so overpowering is the effect.'

He at once replied, 'Look! That is the meaning of it! He comes! The prince, the prince! I looked, and my eyes rested on him. He was clothed in garments of spotless purity, whiter than the snow on top of the mountains. Following in his train were thousands of the bright ones, and all moving on towards the temple, to engage in the worship of the great and mighty spirit.

All this appeared to me much like that which in some measure might be seen on earth, and everything around me seemed so real: the rocks, the trees, the hills, the valleys clothed with beautiful green—all so lovely, and yet so substantial, that at times, as we proceeded, I could not help imagining it to be but a dream—some vision crossing my brain! Was I mad? Was I still on the earth? Ah, no, no for here beside me was my venerable friend, clothed in his robes of white; and here too, was my beloved wife, with heaven's lustre on her brow, talking to me in the old and oft-remembered tones, and with the same familiar features and form.

These thoughts had just passed away when I observed the prince drawing nigh to us. At first I felt impelled to rush towards him and throw myself at his feet; but a sense of unworthiness coming on me, I drew back. He saw me, however, and coming up to me he clasped me in his arms, exclaiming, 'Father, suffer thus much from me. Thou art welcome! All heaven shouteth for joy that thou art come home. Come, my father, come, let us walk up to the temple that we may worship the great and good, the almighty father.'

We walked side by side till we reached the centre, as it seemed to me, of the vast and magnificent building. Looking around me I saw thousands of golden seats, representing animals I had never seen before. Their eyes were lighted up with fire, while the scales which covered their bodies displayed thousands of ever-varying tints. The wings of these animals formed the seats, on which sat multitudes of the blessed. These figures were so beautifully, so ingeniously constructed, that I took them to be living creatures, but I discovered later they were not so, but works of heavenly art—instruments of praise! And as the prince walked on, ten thousand of these wafted their halleluiahs till the gloriously ravishing concord of sounds died away in the far distance.

My old and esteemed friend, the Egyptian priest, officiated at the altar which stood under the great dome; and at the conclusion of the service, the prince mounted the steps and spoke to the vast multitude assembled before him. I will not attempt to give you an adequate description of this discourse, but I may say that nothing I had ever listened to could be compared to it. It concluded by an appeal, full of love and compassion, on behalf of his fallen brethren in darkness, while he called on this one and that to undertake the mission of love.

'Go down to them', he said, 'and cast forth your influence on these poor darkened, enchained brethren, that they may be lifted up from their dismal condition, and become partakers with you of light and love. How can we be happy while thousands of souls, precious in the sight of the great spirit, are still the denizens of the dark caverns, cursing their God, cursing themselves, not knowing that He is forever willing to draw them away from their darkness into His great light.'

When Jesus had finished speaking to the multitude of bright beings, he descended from the steps of the altar in the centre of the great hall, and moved away followed by a large retinue, and I was left to gaze at greater length upon the wonders of this vast building, so much greater in size than anything ever constructed upon the surface of the earth.

The great central hall is used only for worship, while in four smaller halls which surround it (I say 'smaller', though truth to tell these also are enormous by earth standards), subjects of philosophy and science are introduced for the benefit of those assembled. There you will find that the nationalities of earth are, to a certain extent, still maintained by those who meet there—Greek meeting with Greek, Hindu with Hindu, Hebrew with Hebrew, and so on. Here we find them mutually receiving and imparting truth in connection with such subjects as space, the conditions and peculiarities of other worlds (not now looked at dimly by mortal eyes, and with the hazy imaginations of spirits in the body, but as realities—places which many of them have visited), and many other matters peculiar to life in the spirit world: subjects far above the comprehension of men, however high in culture or genius, who are still clothed in mortal bodies.

The stones forming the great building I am trying to describe are not composed of dark dense material, such as those used on earth. They may be likened to your precious stones, but all of a far, far brighter nature, and yet still material substance. The columns are transparent as crystal, and dazzlingly bright, so much so, that were mortal eyes to look upon them, they would at once be blinded; and oftentimes, indeed, they are dazzling to the eye of spirit. As we gaze of these beautiful columns, there appears a never-ceasing change of colours—in rainbow-like fashion. But greater far than all these qualities, when a spirit looks into them he sees reflected his own self, his own thoughts. Let one of the poor, darkened souls of the spirit world but glance upon these ever-pure columns, and he would fly in terror at the sight. The temple is surrounded by such columns.

The inside walls of the temple are made from various metals, finer in their composition than those of earth. Both stones and metals may be termed material, but yet their nature is spiritual.

The floors of the halls are inlaid with the finest marbles, on which are portrayed in strange figures human passions—the whole symbolical of the treading of such passions beneath the feet of those who enter therein. There are also many strange figures delineated on the masonry supporting the domes of the five halls, and these are connected with man's earthly life.

The altar, or sacrificial form of worship is adopted to suit those who had in their earth life been accustomed to such a mode. Indeed, such sacrificial forms were peculiar to almost all nations till the prince came. There is no harm in the use of these forms. Many a precious night have I spent beside the altar in the sacred grove. And it is to be considered by you that we in the spirit world who, in our earth-life, were accustomed to these things, form the vast majority of those who have entered into spirit-life; and is it at all unreasonable that the modes of thought and worship of this majority should still exist in the spirit-life? When you come hither, all these things will be clear to you. You will find no fault with the arrangement.

There is nothing wrong in those of the same nation fraternising, so that they do not rest contented with that, to the neglect of their duty—which is to endeavour to uplift from the dark caverns of Hades our poor fallen brethren who are still enshrouded in darkness.

2

Hafed describes the spirit world

Having told you something of the temple itself, let me now speak of the surrounds and immediate neighbourhood of the great building. The ground on which it stands is no mere grassy knoll, but a grand and elevated swell of mountainous table-land, whose beautiful sloping sides and terraces are adorned with the richest vegetation. Round the building, and skirting off in every direction, are walks bordered by trees of gigantic size, far far surpassing those of earth (which are but dwarfs when compared with them), and laden with a foliage beautifully diversified in its colouring. Casting the eye down the slopes of the hill, the scene presents to the view of the enraptured beholder, one grand collection of all the colours of nature, and all this is to decorate the winding paths which lead to the gates of the great temple, in which the nations assemble to worship the high and the holy one—the invisible God.

The atmosphere around is ever fresh with the sweet fragrance distilled from the flowery fields, and inhaled at every step by the blest ones who tread these heavenly paths. Here too, may be seen horses and other animals gambolling over the lovely lawns and rich meadows, while myriads of birds, clothed in beauty, are warbling their notes of thanksgiving and praise to the creator.

But the scene is not composed altogether of beautiful woods and flowery meads. At the base of the hill flows a river of the purest water, fed by numerous silvery cascades from the rocky cliffs above, and in the neighbourhood of the temple are many small lakes, in which may be seen multitudes of tiny but lovely fishes dancing about, hither and thither amid the crystal waters, creating interest, delight, and instruction to thousands of little children from earth-life, who are running about the banks, under the care of their heaven-appointed guardians. And here also are to be seen many of the sages of old, walking about absorbed in study and reflection, while here and there you may observe a pair of re-united fond hearts, recounting to each other their experiences of the past life, and reviewing them in the light of the present. There again are to be seen some spirits newly admitted to this paradise of bliss, eagerly gazing on all that meets their enraptured vision.

Had I been told that this was heaven itself I could not, when I entered, have been more satisfied—so beautiful to my senses did everything appear; but man's desires cannot rest in mere enjoyment—he must exercise the faculties with which he is endowed. Accordingly, when my old friend Issha the Egyptian, discoursed with me of the work in which he had been engaged, I too felt a strong desire to traverse the kingdoms of the Lord and visit other planets far away in space.

Here ancient philosophers, as was their wont, still cast their eyes toward the heavens, to discover new beauties in the rolling worlds. At one time these philosophers indulged in many a fanciful speculation concerning the heavenly bodies; now they need speculate no more, for they have visited those worlds, and discovered what they are composed of. They find them inhabited by intelligent beings all as good, and many of them far superior, morally, to those of earth. I myself, in the course of my various missions in the spirit-life, have visited some of these worlds, and I found that the intelligent beings living on them, far excel, in every way, the inhabitants of earth. Many of these beings, having thrown off the material body, have been here too. They pass away from their bodies, not alas; as you do on earth, but as in a sleep, and that not until they are ready to go.

There is no death in the childhood of these races—all come to maturity, and then pass away. It would be well with the earth were its peoples in such a condition. In the worlds I refer to, there is no transgression of God's laws, and consequently there is no suffering—no pride bringing with it those direful results so frequently presented to you on earth; but all are under the loving sway of one great head, and all are subject to the great king (Jesus) who reigns over all. There is no one there envying another's superiority—no one lording it over another, but all are on an equal footing; and why? Because *love* reigns in every heart—each one loves his neighbour as he does himself. And yet these happy and holy beings die—they pass away from the body into spirit-life; not amid grief and lamentation, as is the case with you on earth; but, the indications of the change being well known, it becomes the occasion of joy and gladness to all around—in fact, a jubilee.

When I look back and consider the teachings on this subject contained in the sacred books of Persia and of the Hebrews, I am amazed—I can but term them foolishness. Both Persian and Hebrew scriptures teach that but for the sin there would have been no death. But in the worlds I am speaking of there is no sin, and yet there is still death: certainly not that death with which we are acquainted, with all its painful and terrible accompaniments, but still the parting of the spirit from the body—from the material to the spiritual

Compared with some of these worlds, earth is an atom of dust on an apricot to the apricot itself. Had the inhabitants of earth continued to exist without death, where would you have been? Choke full, with hardly space to breathe in. Death must come; and it comes, in these worlds as in yours, to all in due time. So has it been in the past, and so will it ever be, as long as man is a sojourner on earth's surface. How long his sojourn, none can tell.

Now permit me before I go further, to say something concerning the animals in spirit-life. Take the animals of your world, study them, set them in order, from the smallest insect to the largest and strongest beast, and you will have before you a subject worthy of your deepest consideration. In each and all you will observe a certain amount of instinct or intellect corresponding to their varied structures. You will see the ant, a very small creature, building his house with skill, and displaying forethought by laying up in store provender for the coming winter. Here you have exemplified one of the most important features of man as a rational being.

Then look at the little mole, and the larger beaver, both exhibiting in some measure the powers of engineering and building in man. Take again, the spider, and you have the skilful, industrious weaver; for as the fishermen of earth construct nets to catch fish, so do these little animals weave their nets to entrap the unwary fly. Then on earth you have your birds of passage: these may be called the mariners of the sky. Even in the fish of the sea you may perceive something familiar to that which meets your eye amongst men; for here is one who, finding a shell vacated by another, therein takes up his abode, and keeps it. Indeed, bring all the various classes of animals, with their varied its and habits, under your observation, and you will find that all these are developed in mankind—each and all form part and parcel of man; so that when he leaves the body to go into the spirit world, he carries with him the instincts or intellect of all classes of the animal creation.

But here we must look at another point—that is, the differences existing in animals as regards instinct or intellect. You will find that some animals moving over the surface of the earth, having their spines in a horizontal position; others, again, not exactly so, but varying from horizontal to an angle of forty-five degrees; while man alone walks upright. It is in this we find the cause of diversity in animals. The solar rays, giving forth electricity, strike down on man's brain, and thence down through his spine, in an unbroken stream, while in the lower animals, these rays striking on the spine from an angle of forty-five degrees to the horizontal get broken up or scattered.

Seeing that all these instincts of the lower animals were needed on earth in order that there should be completeness in mankind, it was also necessary that these should be carried by man into the spirit world; for if you set him down in a paradise such as I have recently described without these instincts, he will find himself in a wilderness—you deprive him of that which goes to make up his happiness. But no, here we have all that you have on earth—all much superior in character, but all in strict correspondence with that which exists with you in the material world, and of which you are cognisant by your bodily senses.

I have in my spirit-life traversed the various districts of the spirit-land. I have visited places of all sorts, some of which might have been termed hell, but to me all appeared beautiful. Here the eye rests fondly on nature's variegated fields of floral verdure, and there the little streamlet wimples along its rocky bed; here we have the majestic rivers pouring their rolling waters into the quiet and pellucid lakes, that mirror in their deep bosoms the image of the passers-by; and there, sweet music lends its powerful aid to awaken hardened, benighted, dark souls, to lift their eyes upwards towards Him who can dispel the thick clouds which enshroud them—to Him who is the source of all light, without whose loving beams they are powerless to burst through the pride-bound gate that shuts them out from the companionship of the truly happy.

3

Different spheres of habitation

Having spoken of the connection which existed between man and the lower animals, showing that man is the complete animal; that each animal is a link, and that all form one grand chain, of which man is the head link; that all had more or less reason, according to their several organisations, and that reason was the great spiritual principal in man. Let me now confine my remarks to the subject of man in spirit-life, and let me recur my own experience after parting from the body.

On waking up I felt as if I had come out of a troubled dream. The past few hours appeared to me as a sort of dreamy unreality, and yet I knew that that which had taken place was altogether real—a fact—not to be set down as mere fancy. For a time I felt in that dreamy, hazy-like condition. I began, gradually, to consider; I could observe no difference in myself—not even in the clothing with which I was covered. This is something for you to think about. Whence came these clothes? The spirits did not bring them along with me in the spirit-land. How then? But as the scales fell from my eyes—as I began to realise the fact of my translation, I perceived that though my clothing was like that which covered me on earth, it was not the same. I then began to examine my frame, and in that likewise all appeared as usual: there were my hands, my feet, the shape of my body—the very bones—aye, even the swollen blue veins in my arms and hands, and the nails on my finger-ends—all there! But as I wondered and gazed, all became transparent—there was no density in that on which I looked.

I continued to look at myself and my surroundings, and as I looked I ruminated: Is this then, the grand change that has absorbed the attention of philosophers of all ages and countries? Has the veil at last been drawn aside? Now I see things as they really are. Now I stand out in enduring form, solid and more substantial than are the everlasting rocks: these may, in the lapse of ages, crumble into sand; the mortal body may be dissolved into the elements, and be blown hither and thither by the winds, but here is the indestructible body. Man may—and, alas! how often does he—destroy his earthly body; but this spiritual frame shall never be destroyed. O glorious change! From earth with all its sins and sorrows and sickness, to heaven with its enduring rest and peace and joy!

Thus I meditated, and thus I wonderingly mused, and as I did so, the truth, like rays of light, darted into me. That which I had been accustomed to look on as substantial realities, even earth's great rocks and mountains and seas, now appeared to me but as shadows when contrasted with the grand and magnificent objects on which my vision rested. It was not, however, until the forms of my wife and son, with my beloved parents, and friends and companions long passed away, stood round about me, that I realised the fact of my transition—that I had indeed passed from death to life—from the mortal to the immortal. Besides, I could now perceive the hearts of those dear ones with whom I came in contact. Of course I do not refer to the bodily heart—that great force-pump of the blood (if you carefully examine that blood you will perceive the magnetic spark so necessary to the proper action of the heart)—not that, but something different from and yet corresponding with that important organ of the body—I mean the spirit heart—the affections—the thoughts projected from the innermost of the inner man. Observe, the spirit has what I may call an inner spirit. If you could but understand it! You look on man encased in his wondrous human form, and you behold in that form only the temple of the spirit—the dwelling-place of the man— so beautifully adapted to all his requirements as an inhabitant of earth; you turn your eyes to the spirit-form—the heavenly body; but that is not the man—that is not the ALL, there is in that celestial body the INNER MAN—the thinking, feeling, acting being, the DIVINE PART—the eternal indestructible offspring of God. Do you see it? There is, first the body; then the spirit; and then the divine part: all these go to make up the individual, the man.

In the earth-life, the inner or God-part—the soul—may be so obliterated, so defaced by worldliness and sin, that there seems to be nothing left but the spirit. Man, by transgression of law, shuts out God. Coming here in such a condition he is driven—he cannot help being driven—into the dark regions of despair: there he abides without hope, and abandoned of God as he thinks. But still there is hope, for he is not forgotten: the angels of mercy and love are on the watch for an opening by which they may operate on the inner part of this darkened immortal; and when this opening does take place, as a result of the discipline undergone—when this little chink appears, then is the door thrown open for the influence of the ministers of love and truth; the light flows into the dark cells of this being, gradually and slowly at first, but ever increasing; and as the light comes in, so does the degraded one emerge from his miserable condition, and rises—ever rises upward and onward. We, in our loved missions, are ever on the watch in such cases, and when the opportunity occurs, it is our joy and delight to work for goodness and truth—to lift the poor helpless, hopeless one up out of the foul waters of his sins to God's pure stream of truth, and thus to float him on into our sphere of light and love. In those who come here in a renewed condition, the divine part of their nature becomes the thinking, acting part, and as they continue in this course, so do they become more and more like unto Jesus who is the image of the invisible God.

The spirit world comprises of many differing spheres, in which spirits, in accordance with their condition, find a suitable habitation. Though there are many who term them 'spheres', I prefer to call them places; countries, similar to those of earth. And inasmuch as the various tribes of men on earth (as I said before) are drawn together into nations or countries, so is it with man in spirit-life—the various classes or conditions find their respective localities. One man of your earth may have a love for the gay and delicate flowers that decorate the fields and gardens. Another takes a wider range, and takes delight in grand and beautiful scenery, and his soul revels amid the mountains whose snow-capped tops pierce into the heavens. Another, amid the thundering roar of dashing waters pouring from the cliff above to the dark depths below, loves to contemplate the rainbow hues of the cascade. Others, again, prefer quiet solitude in the dark gloomy paths of the forest, that their hearts may rise in aspiration to God; while another class find their greatest pleasure on the waters in the bright and beautiful sunshine. Even so is it in the world of spirits. There is one who loved the beautiful flowers of earth, and he finds his loved and lovely treasures in their celestial beauty much more lovely than he ever dreamt of. Here too, there is enough to satisfy the admirer of nature in her grander aspects, of mountains and valleys—of flood and field. Here the joyous waters fall from the rocky heights in a tide of music, at once gratifying the eye and ravishing the ear of him whose soul loves to find pleasure amid such scenes. Then again we have our grand old woods and their quiet solitudes, through which the contemplative man may walk and meditate on the great spirit, and on all his wonderful ways and works—how all is so beautifully fitted to the necessities of the creature by the all-wise and almighty creator, and how all become, by his arrangement, sweet ministers to man. There too, on the banks of a beautiful lake, whose silver waters ripple under the beams of heavenly light, we have great gatherings of the lovers of music, whose songs of praise, reverberating on the distant rocks, come back in harmonious echoes across the waters, filling their hearts with gladness, love, and peace.

Such scenes as I have been describing, are only adapted to man in a truly moral condition; for where I am all are God-like. It is different in the dark places of the spirit world; there men are still under the dominion of the animal part of their nature; their God-like part is still buried up, over-grown with weeds, with no eye, no ear for heavenly things. Not until these choking weeds are torn away can the spirit be made to feel that there are treasures around him which he may possess. When, however, the hindrances are removed, he finds a place suitable to his moral condition. Painters, artisans, philosophers—all find in spirit-life their varied wants and aspirations fully met by the wise providence of the great ruler.

4

A search for Xerxes in the dark regions

Let me now give you some account of the rescue of one of my own countrymen from the dark prison-house in the spirit world which I have just spoken of.

He had been one of the kings of Persia, and was named Xerxes—the Great, as he has been called. If to be the proudest tyrant that ever ruled over a nation entitles him to be called great, then great he was; but it assuredly was at the expense of his people's happiness and national ruin. Speaking as a Persian, and from an earthly point of view, he was one that ought to have been trampled beneath the feet of every patriotic man. Why do I say this? Because, while his predecessors on the throne had striven hard to promote the happiness and prosperity of the people, he, the vain—glorious, heartless despot, robbed his own nation, and the nations that were subject to him, of their wealth, and prodigally spent it on the silly decoration of his soldiers. He cared not where it came from, nor by what means; but gold he would have.

He seems to have had all his pleasure in the ostentatious display of soldiers clothed in the most gorgeous apparel; and it was no uncommon sight to see the armour of many of those who followed him to battle inlaid with pearl, and sparkling with precious stones. What foolishness. But it has always been thus with the proud and vain tyrants of the earth. Pride produces folly, and folly brings forth ruin. He was never satisfied unless he had some monarch bending in the dust before him (I am now speaking as a mortal). He marched against nation after nation, subjecting them to his tyrannic sway, and demanding their wealth to be laid at his feet. His thirst for gold, to satisfy the demands of his vain—glorious shows, was insatiable. But the Greeks were too much for him. Some of their smaller states submitted as tributaries, but Athens and Sparta stood out against him, determined not to crouch before this tyrant, with his innumerable hosts.

Mad—like as it appeared, they were resolved to humble his pride. Xerxes and his great army marched against Greece. They thought not of defeat. What could these hundreds do against his thousands? But these hundreds of Greeks withstood the mighty hosts of the Persians and their tributaries, who were over-thrown, and driven back with great slaughter. Xerxes, and the remnants of his great army, in their disastrous retreat, arrived at the Hellspont, but found the Bridge of Boats, which he had caused to be built on his advance, destroyed by a storm. Enraged at this misfortune, he cruelly ordered the builders of the bridge to be crucified. But this was not all, for the Athenians had succeeded in burning the greater portion of his immense fleet. It may easily be imagined that few of the ill-fated expedition returned with Xerxes to Persia. But I think the Persians were as much to blame as was their king for this expedition and its terrible result. He went back a second time, and again met with a disastrous defeat. He was at Sue, when an officer of his guards, who had deserted to the Greeks, but had returned to Persia, assassinated him.

In my early earth-life I had read of Xerxes and his conquests, as recorded in our historical books, in which he was held up to view as one of the greatest of Persia's kings; but our writers were blind to the fact that the means whereby he acquired his so-called greatness were dishonest, and his vainglorious warlike parade a proof of his folly. In reading about this king and his ill-fated expedition, I felt deeply impressed by it, and pitied my fellowmen of other countries, who were obliged to contribute a considerable amount of wealth for the expenses of war. And not only this, but there were even some who lavishly expended their people's wealth in keeping up a regular body of troops in time of peace. It had also been the custom in Persia to keep up their soldiers in a splendour that was gratifying to the eye in time of peace, but worse than useless in active warfare. But that foolishness of course had been abandoned.

As I have said, I felt deeply impressed by reading the history of this king, and when I came here (to the spirit world), I made inquiry after him, with the intention, if I found him still in darkness, to do what I could to rescue him. But no one could give me any information about him. Even some of our greatest and wisest philosophers were at fault. These sent me hither and thither through many different districts of the spirit world, yet all in vain.

Determined to discover the object of my search, I traversed many a place, or country, as you would say, without success. My heart, however, was set on this one thing, and I persevered in my search, but could find no clue by which I could fall in with him whom I sought. At length the thought struck me, 'Why not make inquiry of the prince? All are under his rule. He should know how to direct me in my search.' Accordingly I resolved that, when next he appeared in the great temple for worship, I would inquire of him. This opportunity occurred on the day following. Before he ascended the throne, I told him how I was impressed concerning the condition of that poor soul, and of the many fruitless efforts I had made to discover him. He turned to me and said, 'Father, (he always calls me father), he whom you so earnestly seek was consigned to the dark dungeons for the injuries he inflicted on his fellow-men. You will find his place in the Book of Memory at the porch of the temple. He is a fit subject for you to raise from darkness to light. Go and do it, and a bright, a blazing star will sparkle on your forehead.'

I did as I was commanded. I looked on the Great Book of Memory. While engaged in my search therein, I found that some of those who had been my companions amongst the Magi were far down in the spirit world, while others, whom I reckoned bad men, were in condition much higher up. I pondered, and saw how apt man in mortal form is to blunder on this point.

I had never travelled far from the blessed land into which I had been ushered when I left the body; but now, I felt I was bound to relinquish it for the time being, and be take myself to places far down in the spirit world—to those dark regions, the abode of benighted spirits. I told my old friend, the Egyptian, what I intended to do, and he at once said, 'Come my son, I know the way; and we shall together undertake this mission: we were companions on earth, and, though not of the same religion, we worshipped the same God, who has ever been good to us; and now we shall go forth together on this mission of mercy on behalf of His despairing ones.'

As we travelled down (using an earthly phrase) we became witnesses to many a pitiful sight, which brought tears to our eyes, and grief to our hearts. Multitudes of our fellow-men were seen by us, many of them herding together, but all surrounded by spiritual darkness, impenetrable as the solid rock. Poor miserable souls, they could not perceive us; they seemed to be encrusted all over; but our clear vision could pierce through all, and what to them appeared dark and dismal, to us was beautiful in refulgent light.

After traversing many strange places, we were led, under the guidance of our blessed star (the same spirit who directed our steps to Bethlehem), to him who we desired to find. We found him amongst the solitary ones in the lowest sphere, thousands of whom wandered about unknowing and, to each other, unknown—each one in utter solitude. To us, the sight was more sad and distressing than any we had witnessed. Amongst the masses of the benighted ones in the second sphere, or condition, there was at least some relief, for they, though moving amidst darkness, could yet perceive each other, and find a kind of pleasure in combining to plan and work out mischief on earth. Hence the myth about a personal devil still taught by some. But it is here where the real evil ones—mischief makers—are to be found, and whom we find much more difficult to raise than the solitary wanderers.

We found him who once bore the name Xerxes, wandering about in all his pride, clad in his gorgeous robes, and, as it were, in deep meditation, studying his favourite subject—war. On a nearer approach we found him wrapped so closely in his cloak of pride, that we failed to break through the dense atmosphere—we just wanted to throw in, as a preliminary operation, a little light upon him, so that he might realise, to some extent, our presence. Often we tried, and as often we failed, to produce the desired condition by which we might rescue the poor soul. At last we met with a female spirit, who had been trying for years to accomplish the same end. She, like us, was in a superior state, and had seen him who had not only been her king, but her husband, enter the spirit world a poor solitary soul, and she pitied him, for she had loved him as a wife in his power and grandeur on earth, and she loved him in the spirit world in his poverty. She appeared a good and loving soul; and this was seen in her coming from her happy home to those dreadful caverns of the despairing ones, to seek for her lost husband—to raise him from darkness to light. She had banished herself, as it were, from the society of the good, and mingled with the evil (though these could not affect her), so that she might rescue him whom she loved.

Along with this loving spirit, we made an effort to throw in our combined influence on the poor wanderer—being instructed by my friend Issha and by this female how to proceed, for the method was quite new to me. Our joint effort resulted at last in the breaking up of the dark cloud which enveloped the poor man. He seemed astonished, and wondered what was wrong with him. This was something new in his miserable experience. He was startled—moved in soul; and looking around, he saw some of the spirits in similar condition, but he could not yet see us. He attempted to run from those he saw, and of whom he was evidently afraid, on which my friend Issha, remarked, 'When you see them startled, and try to run from others, you may calculate on success.'

From time to time we watched him; at length he began to be conscious of our presence, and casting his eyes on our robes, glittering with stars, his pride appeared to drop from him, gradually, until he stood naked before us.

On discovering his loving wife, a smile came over his countenance; but quickly it passed away, and he cried out, 'Go from me! I am not worthy of thee; fly, O fly from me, I who once despised thee!'

Whereupon Issha said to him, 'Do not drive that kind, loving soul away, who has just opened your eyes, that have long been closed.'

'Oh,' he said, 'far rather would I wander on in my solitary course than look upon you. Are ye gods who thus come to me?' Has she come hither to witness against me of all my evil deeds?'

'No, poor soul, we are not gods, but men like yourself. Beside me stands one of your own countrymen. We are not here to accuse you—we come to bring you back, by the orders of our prince, to light and love, to goodness and truth. Turn not your eyes to the dismal scenes around you, but lift them to the bright and glorious land beyond!'

He seemed deeply moved. 'Do you repent?' said Issha.

'I do indeed repent in bitterness of soul my earthly course; I am verily guilty, for even in my dark and dreary prison house, how often have I refused to admit that I, Xerxes, the great king, was a fit subject for punishment—how often have my curses recoiled on my own proud and rebellious heart! Alas! what shall I say? Have I not deserved this and a thousand-fold more, for all the misery, and ruin, and death which I, to gratify my pride, brought on my fellow-men?' O great and good one—Thou who reignest over all—Thou who art just in all thy ways, have mercy on me a poor, naked, miserable offender against thy holy laws, and forgive me my sins, for they are great.'

Thus he lamented, and thus he prayed. It was enough. He was now alive to his true condition. The kind female spirit never left him; while day after day we came into communion with him, and endeavoured, through the opened avenues of the spirit, to throw in some new truth—something to lead him on in an upward course.

We continued our attention to this poor spirit until we got him past the stage previously referred to, where spirits combine together for evil ends; for once past that point, there need be no fear of them going back. He now began to see us as we really were; and, step by step, we saw, with pleasure, the uprising of this man towards goodness and truth, who had once been one of the earth's noted tyrants—a worker of evil. Now he is one of the good, at all times anxiously desirous to do for others what we did for him.

The kind and loving spirit, she who had spent so long a time in watching over him when imprisoned in darkness, is ever with him, and accompanies him in all the errands of love he undertakes; and many in the land of the happy have now reason to bless the day when they met with the spirit who is known on earth as Xerxes the Great.

5

An address on spiritualism

Now I wish to speak to you on the claims of spiritualism. I am addressing those whom I may designate the pioneers of the grand army already on the march for the coming conflict; and yet, in styling you pioneers, I am not unmindful of many who have gone before you who might well bear the noble name, as propagators of the truth—the grand science of spiritual communion, for indeed it is THE science of all sciences. Were your professed scientists only sincere in their desire to arrive at a solution of the difficulties that encompass the investigation—were they to go about it in the same spirit which they manifest in other matters, the truth, in all its beauty, would soon burst upon them, that all things, everything they are perceptive of—the entire universe of material worlds rolling in space, with all the multitudinous hosts of intelligences that inhabit them—the still greater spirit world, the dwelling-place of the immortals—have sprung from the great, ever-present, all-wise source of all things, our father God, the infinite spirit.

Why should these philosophers start back from inquiry because of the seeming simplicity of the methods by which many of the manifestations of spirit power are produced? Conduct such as many of them exhibit is altogether unlike that which we expect to see in the true philosopher. They are false to science. Philosophically considered, what matters it whether signals are made by taps or raps on an article of furniture, or whether, as is not now uncommon, a voice is heard from an invisible agent? Is not the despised tap as much a product of law as is the sound of the human voice? Let these men seek for the origin of these sounds in the right spirit, and they will be rewarded. The great philosophers who lived in long past ages of the world did not despise the study of this subject (for, be it remembered, this is no new thing); they searched with all diligence till they found, and though some failed, they did not hesitate to conclude that these sights and sounds had a supernatural origin; others, again, were more privileged, for they opened their hearts at once to the great and glorious truth, that heaven was indeed thrown open to their longing souls.

And is it not a gladsome thing to know that we who have been so long away can come back and speak to you as we used to do when inhabiting the mortal body? that the gates of the unseen world, which so many imagine to be fast closed, are not so, but stand wide open? that the loved ones whom so many think are torn away from you by what you term 'cruel death' the father, whom you venerated; the mother whom you never can cease to love, the husband, the wife, the brother and sister, and the little darlings that clung to you in loving embraced— that these can and do come back again, and make known their presence, telling you of their life in spirit, and of the blessed reception that awaits the wise and good of all ranks and of every nation?

But there are some who are afraid to look at this subject which you call spiritualism, they are dreadfully afraid lest it overthrow their cherished theological systems. And what is this that stands like a huge lion in the way of these timid souls? To such I would say: go to your leaders (churchmen) who pretend to know so much about the spirit world and the life behind the veil, ask them to tell you something concerning it, and they will say, with some show of mystery, that there are but two places in the life beyond, between which there is a great impassable gulf; that when the spirit leaves his body he is lost to the world, and will never come back till the great day when the earth shall be burned up with flaming fire, and then, encased in the resurrected shell, he comes forth for judgment. You will find that the great mass of these blind and blinding leaders of the people have no certain knowledge of the subject to impart to the poor inquirer. Some of them will tell you that the spirit of the just 'sleep in Jesus' till the resurrection morning when that comes none can tell, and again, almost in the same breath, they will speak of the deceased as in the enjoyments of heaven, and 'present with the lord:' while in regard to all others, they do not hesitate to consign them to the regions of lost souls, there to abide until the resurrection, when, re-united to their mortal bodies, and judgment passed, their anguish is intensified by the junction, and ever increases in intensity to all eternity!

Ah me! How the systems of men darken and disfigure the simple truth! Not come back! Where have they got this notion? It is but a thin partition that divides the two worlds, the one is no great distance from the other; and there is no impassable gulf, dark and dismal, separating earth from the paradise of the good, or even from the dark places of the poor, self-impris-oned, self-degraded soul. Believe it or not. We can and we do bridge over this supposed gulf this valley of death; for quick as a thought we are with you,—the wish is barely formed, when we are present to bless you.

There are some, however, who have no belief at all in spirit-life; they will tell you they have no proof of such a life; that it may or it may not be for aught they know; that the death of the body is seemingly the end of man, that the great and the good of all time, with all their virtues, with all their bright and glorious attainments, go down with the poor casket to the dust of the earth! There are some too, who, in addition to this, doubt or disbelieve the existence of God—the grand parent of all—the great spirit, who liveth and provideth for every one. This perversity, though deep and painful to many of you, must not hinder you in your efforts to set the truth before them. These men are the blinded victims of the false theologies which have prevailed in the world—see that you who have the truth, make its light shine before them. No God! No life after so-called death? Man an orphan—a passing shadow? No, no, a thousand times no! Though such a one may entertain the dismal thought, though he believe not in an immortal state, let me tell him, that he, even he goes forth in spirit into the world of spirits, while this wearied body reclines on its welcome bed of rest; and although, on awakening, he is unconscious of the fact, nevertheless as a spirit he has gone forth, and taken part in things better and brighter and more glorious than he and his vaunted philosophy ever dreamt of.

But some of these may say: If this great and good spirit is all you say He is, why does He permit evil to raise its head? Why allow the wicked to triumph over the good? To crush truth and subject its adherents to torture and death—permitting evil men even to lay hands on the innocent—to bring disease and death on thousands and tens of thousands of helpless, innocent children? Why is this? Well, they are the victims—sacrificed—martyrs in the cause of truth and goodness—suffering on account of others. When the great prophet of the Hebrews said that the iniquities of the fathers fall on their children to the third and fourth generation he uttered the truth—a truth which cannot be denied: Do you not see them suffering from diseases inherited from their forefathers—down, down through generations to their source? And these poor little ones, who should have grown up to be stalwart men, and healthy, beautiful women, strong in body and mind, and useful to their fellow-men—pass away from their frail house, unfitted for earth, and undeveloped in spirit for the duties on this side. This is not God's work. It is in opposition to his laws. His will is, that, by the discipline of earth, they should be brought to maturity as men and women, and thereby become, when they leave the body, fitted for the employments and joys of the spirit world.

But from the beginning the innocent and the good have been the victims—slain because of the guilty and evil-minded. Behold in Jesus of Nasareth, my prince, a martyr to the truth which he taught: the holy and the just condemned and crucified, and the robber Barabbas set free! It has ever been so—truth is crucified, and iniquity is honoured.

As I have already said, spiritualism is no new thing. There were always some who knew that mortals could communicate with the world of spirits—could walk and talk with angels; and some of those who were so privileged, who got thereby the glorious light into their souls, built up systems of theology, but which are now rotten—falling to pieces! Why? Because their adherents deny the very foundation of their own creed—communion with the dear ones who have gone before. Just think of it. Fathers and mothers, to you I speak. Is not the truth gladdening to your hearts, that the loved ones who have passed over can still come back—that you can still communicate with them, even those bright little prattlings that sat on your knees, that fondled you with their tiny fingers, and with pure lips kissed you on the cheek? And you had to part with them, and the bitter thought arose: They are lost—lost for ever! Ah, no, it is not so; banish the thought. They visit you; they come to bless you—to watch over you, as much as we the aged do—we who have long, long ago crossed over the stream. These dear ones come to your hearths with their chains of roses to enwreath you, and to shed down on you the sweet perfume of the heavenly land in which they dwell.

You (spiritualists) are, my friends, having the finger of scorn pointed at you because of your adherence to the truth of spirit-communion; and you have to a certain extent to become martyrs, by laying bare the truth to your fellow-men. But had you done so in past times, you would have been treated in a very different manner. 'Draw back your words or die!' Such would have been the ordeal in days gone by. They thought to kill the apostle of truth—to stamp him out of existence: in their bigoted blindness they but set him free. I knew something in my earth-life of this kind of opposition. Be not afraid. Be bold for the truth. Take Jesus the prince, as your pattern. He was never afraid to proclaim the most unwelcome truths before a whole nation; nor did he hesitate on every fitting occasion to show his great power, in giving sight to the blind, hearing to the deaf, health to the sick—in making the lame to walk, and even bringing back the spirit to the cast-off body. He had these spiritual gifts without measure, and he exercised the power wherever and whenever he perceived that good would result therefrom to man.

Go on then, and fear not. We are with you, and present to help you in the declaration of the truth; and as messengers from the great and mighty father, we are ever desirous to give you that which will convince the world that we are with you—that we, who are reckoned dead, are still alive, and live for ever.

If men would only wake up to the lessons imparted to them by heaven's ministering angels, the day would soon come when the churches would be thrown open to them, to go in and proclaim, with trumpet-tongues, the grand, the eternal truths which Jesus uttered. Then would they be able to do the works which he did, and then would his promise be fulfilled. Why should those who are banded together as his followers, and bearing his name, deny his words? Must I answer this question? Since ever man had existence on the earth to the present time, the religious leaders of the people—the priests—neglecting the truth given to them from the spirit world for the benefit of man, have busied themselves in the building up of their theological systems, leaving the poor spirit of man without instruction to fit him for the life on this side. There have been exceptions: but such has been the rule in all ages, and amongst all nations.

These men—these so-called spiritual leaders—and their unthinking followers, may look upon you (spiritualists) as madmen, sneer at you, and mark you for ridicule; but, strong in the light which we have vouchsafed to you, heed them not. No doubt it is a kind of martyrdom hard to bear, but even as Jesus, my prince bore it, so must also you bear it.

'We would disdain.' say other opposers, 'to sit round a table, to see it tilt, and listen to raps!' And so should all reasonable people, were that the only object. They who speak thus forget that such manifestations are but the means to an end—the mode adopted by certain spirits for communion with mortals. And here let me warn those who are now reading this, to give no cause for such objections when assembled at what is termed a circle. Sit down in a reverent, child-like condition of mind, sincerely desiring spiritual food, and you will be ministered to by spirits of the right kind. Having truth for your object, never mind the apparent simplicity of the means by which it is to be obtained. It is surely just as reasonable to give information through the signal of raps, as to do so by controlling the organisation of a man or woman.

But it has ever been that what was considered foolishness, alike by the thoughtless worldling, and the proud philosopher, has turned out to be the very wisdom of God, through the ministration of His messengers. Here is one, a noble boy, who loved his mother dearly, and who was as dearly loved by that mother. He is gone, no one knows whither. Ah! Who may calculate that mother's doubts and fears—who can describe them? She seeks for tidings of the lost one, but no mortal can relieve her breaking heart. At length, someone whispers to her that she may gain information by communion with spirits. She sits down at a table, and here is a medium, through whom spirits can work—it is through this mediumship they can get at the table. Raps are heard. The spirits producing these sounds are asked to spell out their names, (I have often stood by while this was done). A name is given. It is her son's! Then comes question on question, and answer after answer, in relation to the circumstances of his life and of his death. He comforts her. He will be ever near to her until death, and will be at hand to welcome her to the land of light and glory. The mother's anxious soul is at rest. She knows where he is, and how he is, and she longs to meet him in the paradise of the blest. But suppose now that poor woman, in her anxiety, had gone to a priest. 'Can you tell me anything of my lost son?'

'No, no,' he would say. 'Go home and pray to God; it may be that He will give you light.' But as for information regarding her son, he, the so-called servant of God, has none to give her.

Some of us can operate in another way. One who has the power may use the hand of a medium, and give you written communications of great length on various subjects concerning both worlds.

Again, many of you know something of what is termed *direct* writing, and also *direct* drawings—that is, writings and drawings produced without the use of mortal hands, (such as those which David and Jehoram, kings of the Hebrews received), and also of many other modes of communication.

But why need I say more? Walk ye in the steps of the Great Prince, Jesus the Nazarene, and ye will have the gifts which he promised. Then will your churches receive the spirit of him in whom they profess to believe, and then will be ushered in the longed-for golden age, when man and angel will walk together in loving and holy converse.

As I have said, there were some in all ages of the world who knew about these things, and others who made them the subject of investigation and study. Let me then, briefly glance at spiritualism as it was practised in some of the nations in olden times; and this will be done by looking at their various modes of communication.

The peoples of the Far East excelled those of the west in their knowledge of spiritual-intercourse. This, generally speaking, may be ascribed to their habit of long fasting when desirous of communion with the gods—for such they held the spirits to be. This practice of fasting made it much easier to control the medium, and to bring him into the sphere of the controlling spirit. He became as it were, a better tool in the hands of the controller than if he had been full in body and strength. Weakened through long fasting, it is easier for us to work through the medium on all occasions. The Far East became thus celebrated in spiritual knowledge. The powers of their mediums were so full that they could remain for a length of time within the spirit-sphere, and carry back into the mortal state that which they saw and heard in the dwelling places of the gods

Coming westwards and nearer to Persia, we find fasting still practised, though not generally. Nor was it persisted in for any length of time, as in the east, for such a practice was not in accordance with the lessons we taught the people for the preservation of health (I am speaking of the Magi); and my spirit guide gave me no encouragement to those long fasts that injured man's bodily system. When we entered the sacred grove in the early morning, we did no fasting, that we might be fitted to receive all that the great and holy angel of the fire had to impart to us, and through us to the assembled Magi waiting outside the holy place.

In Egypt another mode was adopted. Certain priestesses connected with the temple service were dedicated to the work of communion. These mediums could be consulted only in two places in Egypt. They were kept carefully secluded, and held as devoted to the work. Indeed, so closely were they kept to it that they were seldom off their beds on which they lay in deep trance, and suffered correspondingly in health. The messages were delivered in the trance state. There was also another method. The medium priestess stood at a small table, having a polished silver top, on which her fingers rested, and the inquirer, looking on the clear surface, read or saw thereon that which he sought for. The priests also wore polished stones on their breasts, and the inquirer saw on these the information he wanted, which might be applicable to things of earth, or to those of the spirit world. This latter mode was adopted by the Hebrews—their high priest wearing a breastplate of polished stones, through which messages or information were given to those who sought for such. But the Egyptians did not hide their light, as some did in those olden times. They gave it forth to the benefit of the people. Messages warning of threatened danger were laid before the council of state, so that the government might be prepared for it, or take measures whereby it might be averted. You have a case in point in the story which Moses gives of Joseph—how predicted famine was provided for. Egypt, in this case may be said to have been made the granary of all the neighbouring nations, and much wealth flowed in to her on consequence. The Egyptians afforded more instruction in regard to spiritual matters than any other nation under the sun. None ventured so far as they did in this. The world of spirits, and the condition of spirit-life, were plainly and repeatedly opened up to the people, so that they might be prepared for the inevitable judgement that awaited them at death, by which, if found wanting, they would be hurled into a place of discipline (not into eternal hell), the experiences of which would in due time elevate them — rising higher and higher, until they became gods.

The Grecians were far behind other nations in knowledge pertaining to spirit-communion. They had their oracles, but used them in such a way that much was lost. The Greeks asserted that they received their messages from the marble idols! Not so the Egyptians; theirs (they said) came from the high and holy spirits. As for the Romans, they were very far back in all spiritual knowledge.

The Hebrews were equal to the Persians in this matter of spirit-communion; and, had they lived up to the favours conferred on them, they would have been a grand people indeed. But they were everywhere held in detestation because of their evil deeds.

I cannot speak so freely of spiritualism as it existed after my day; but this I know, that there has never been a time when there were no mediums for spirit-communications. The gift has been often hidden — buried out of sight — by unworthy recipients, afraid that the world should know of it, and they were subjected to suffering and death, but it is high time such unfaithfulness should cease. Why should man any longer go into the spirit world in a condition of doubt, delusion, or darkness, when he may enter in with the light of truth — in the sunshine of knowledge?

There is nothing in this great subject calculated to darken the path of man, but much to enlighten him in his earthly course. Come then friends, be up and doing. See what you can do to raise your fellow-men and fellow-women from the depths of sin and misery into which multitudes of them have sunk. Earth alas! has, still her poor outcast wanderers. I can see them on your busy streets, wandering hither and thither, few caring for their welfare. Shut out from human sympathy, shunned by their own sex, and trampled in the mire by the other, what wonder though these forsaken, desolate souls seek relief in death? Try, my friends, try to do what we are doing in the spirit world. A grand, a noble, and a godlike work it is—to rescue even one of God's offspring from misery.

Think not, however, that your efforts must be confined to mortals. This idea has too long prevailed. You may aid the poor darkened one who seeks to attract your attention at your circles. Drive him not away; he is, as much as you are, the offspring of the great and mighty father, who loveth and careth for all His children alike. That poor wanderer of the spirit world, mourning and groping amid the darkness that enshrouds him, may, by even one kind word uttered at your circle, be guided into the upward path, that will lead him into the brighter spheres of the spirit-realm—into the realisation of the light that ever flows from goodness and truth. Great will be your joy when you cross the river, to find him whom you helped to rise waiting to meet you, to give you a gladsome greeting on your entry into the better land.

Up then, and unfurl the banner of truth. Be not afraid of anything that man may say or do. The way is open; turn not aside, but go forward. We are with you to guide you in your course. Boldly and faithfully pursue that course, and soon will you see the streaks of light, harbingers of the glorious day—the good time predicted in our ancient books, when earth will be one grand scene of love and peace—when all shall acknowledge Jesus the Nazarene as their lord and prince, living under his loving sway, and evermore holding sweet fellowship with the wise and good of all the ages.

Communication

from

HERMES THE EGYPTIAN

Pupil of Issha and Hafed, and a

childhood friend of Jesus

NOTE

This communication from Hermes, a favourite pupil of Issha the old Egyptian priest and Hafed, commences its story at that point in time when Issha had in fact just died.

1

Issha passes into spirit

O what a feeling of complete desolation passed through me as I gazed upon that cold and lifeless corpse which had once been the beloved Issha. So stupefied was I by sorrow that I forgot all I had received from his holy lips. I realised not, that even then he was the possessor of a more glorious body, and an inhabitant of the land of bliss. I cast my eyes on the cold, outstretched form, on the still, placid, marble-like countenance of my beloved teacher—my more than father—and in my anguish asked; Where, O where art thou, my friend, my guide? Why hast thou left me thus in darkness and in doubt? And as I gave vent to my sorrow in bitter lamentation, I fell prostrate on the floor. Where was the god-like-man I could have worshipped—so noble-hearted, so holy in all his ways! And now, as I looked on those well-worn features, the eyes that once shone so bright were dim; the lips whence issued words of wisdom and love, were cold and silent—no smiles to welcome me now—all still and immovable as the solid rock. 'Twas then, in my deep anguish, I cursed my own existence, even the parents that gave me birth, tearing my hair in my madness. Blaspheming, I swore, by all the fiends of hell, there was no God—no future existence—nothing! If there be a God, why am I thus bereft of all that I hold dear?

While thus I madly raved against the God of heaven, my prison cell (for was it not then to me a prison?) was lighted up suddenly. I was amazed; and, as I looked up, there, within a lambent flame, stood one in human form. 'O God!' I cried. 'He has come back to me.' I knelt down on the marble slabs, and, awe-struck, bent my head to the floor. Then heard I the gentle accents of that voice I knew so well. I looked up. 'Twas indeed my beloved father and guide.

I could have touched him; but the form was so gloriously bright, I was afraid. He was clothed in robes transparent as crystal; while his locks were far more beautiful than those of the poor body lying beside me. My eyes were dazzled by the bright, the glorious vision, and I could not continue to look at him. At length he spoke, 'O man, know thyself. Thou art destined to live from age to age, even as He liveth in whose image thou art created. Why hast thou called me back from my blest abode? Why these outbursts of rebellious complaint? Did I not counsel thee, while I was yet with thee in body, that I would, though taken away, be ever near thee in spirit? Did not I give thee sufficient evidence to banish thy doubts—to convince thee that there is no death? Put away then, from thee thy dark and dismal forebodings, and rouse thee to present duty. Have I not told thee that thou wouldst yet be fitted to stand up in this land of Egypt for the pure light, and rid her of her idols, casting aside those foolish mummeries by which the people are blinded; and that the poor of the land would receive bread (spiritual knowledge) from thee?'

His words came back to my mind. I knew not, neither did I care, whether I saw him by the mental or the bodily eye; I knew he lived, and that I listened once more to his gracious voice, and that through life he still would guide me into truth, and guard me from evil, even until I should join him in the mansions of bliss. Why, too, should I have forgotten that which he had so often told me, that thousands of angels are ever watching over and guiding the frail sons of man! He appeared to my astonished eyes so glorious and god-like that in the wonder and awe that took possession of me, I would have worshipped him. But, divining my thoughts, he said, 'See thou do it not. Though my body there is going to dust, and though now clothed in my heavenly body, I am still the same. Hast thou so soon forgotten the lessons I taught thee? Turn to the old writings that have often been the subject of our meditation and study, and consider what they teach, that though man's body goes to the dust whence it comes, the spirit rises into the great world of spirits—goeth back to God its creator. Go forth my son, to the people of Egypt—the downtrodden and benighted people—and in the strength of God and this great truth, and which by my appearance to thee is thus confirmed, proclaim it to them; that so they may be led to consider what they are, children of the great God, who dwelleth not in temples of stone, the work of mens' hands, but who loveth to make His dwelling-place in the hearts of the sons of men, whose throne is in the highest heavens, and whose sceptre stretcheth over all the worlds which He hath made, and which He sustaineth in love and wisdom. Teach them concerning that heavenly land, only to be gained by those of holy life; and that to ensure a happy life beyond, they must live as God would have them live, fearing Him and loving one another. Teach them that, in order to be free from the oppression and tyranny of man, they must seek for the wisdom and knowledge of the true God—having which, they will be free indeed.'

'I have seen my friend and brother Hafed. Write to him, and he will show thee that all I have spoken of is the truth, and worthy of thy deepest consideration. I am here in person—it is I, thy friend—my own true self that now addresseth thee. Therefore, my son, cast aside thy sorrow, and grieve no longer that thou canst not see me in my old worn-out casket; rather rejoice that I have been permitted to come unto thee in my glorious spirit-body, to lead thy mind back to the truth, which thou hadst almost forgotten. Arouse thee! In justice to thyself and to thy poor fellow-men, go forth to the great work; and may the day soon come when light and love and liberty shall spring up, never more to be cut down, over all the earth. Go my son, and be comforted in the great truth of man's immortality.'

So ended his address. While the words fell from his lips, the thought came to me, 'Am I dreaming? Is it indeed my loved friend and father that stands before me?' I rubbed my eyes, and still he was there. The beautiful lips smiled on me; the eyes sparkled as before when he stood at the great altar. How much I felt tempted to prostrate myself in worship before him. His hands, too, as he gently laid them on my head, looked as real as those once did that were even then lying cold and stiff in death, but as they touched me a thrill went all over my body to my finger ends.

When the morning broke, I felt myself a new creature. I went forth, strong in the resolution to expend all my strength of mind and body in behalf of the truth, and never cease my work till I was called home by the great spirit to mingle with the blest above.

2

Hermes leaves Egypt to seek Jesus

While my beloved father and friend had still been of the body, he had made me solemnly promise that I should on no account allow the usual custom of embalming the dead body to take place, but that it should be at once consigned to the dust, there to mingle with its native elements. 'I have no further use for the frail tenement,' he had said—'even as, when I clothe myself in a new garment, and cast aside the old and worn-out one, so let my worn-out body be returned to the ground.' Bearing this in mind, when my brethren proposed to begin the usual ceremonies attendant on embalming, I said, 'No; it cannot be done.'

'Oh, why not?' said they, 'you know it is quite a part of our system; and besides, it is surely right that we should honour one so eminent as he who has been taken away.'

I told them that I had sworn to him that I would bury his body according to his desire. After a long disputation, they consented to take part with me in the work of laying the dead body in the cold earth, where it might dissolve into the elements of which it was composed.

What a solemn procession that was, as it slowly passed over the courts of the ruined temple of Thebes. (It was in ruins because we had no heart, neither had we the means, to repair that which had been ruthlessly broken down; the oppressor's foot was still on the neck of Egypt. No longer were the hungry people fed by her; no longer did she give laws to kings; for, like other great nations of the Earth, she too, had fallen from her high position, and lay enfeebled in the dust). Gorgeous trappings there were none; no ornamental chest with embalmed body of the deceased; but, clothed in his white robe, the body was borne along by the priests, their heads bare and their feet unsandalled, followed by a train of weeping women.

As we proceeded, we sung hymns which had been composed by him whose body we were carrying to the grave, and when we reached the place of burial, I bent my knee in prayer to the great God in the heavens—not now to Him as behind the veil—ah no; for my mind's eye was now open to behold Him as the father of all, who was revealed to us in all his beautiful works in the heaven above and over all the Earth. Slowly and sadly we lowered the body into its resting-place; and while we shovelled the earth back over the grave, there burst upon our ears a strain of glorious music, flowing, as it seemed, from the united voices of ten thousand of the heavenly host. Our souls were enraptured by the celestial harmony, as it filled the air around and above us. We felt, as it were, at the gates of heaven. That was the revival of the priests. 'Harken brother! listen to the music!'

'Yes, yes,' I responded, 'let us join in the celestial chorus,' and our voices and hearts went out in praise.

That day I spoke with a different tongue. I had been accustomed to go through the temple service by mere rote. But now my tongue was loosed. I felt an influence upon me I had never felt before. The priests rallied around me, and thus I spoke, 'As head priest, here I stand before you, brethren of the temple, but from this time henceforth I become a simple man. No longer shall I bend the knee to Isis; no longer is there to me a God behind the veil. The hidden one hath been revealed. 'Why, o why should we longer continue to uphold that which in wrong? Let us go forth and proclaim, throughout the land, that which we know of the true God, of Him who is the creator and upholder of all in heaven and in earth. This is the work enjoined on me by him whose mortal remains we have just laid in the dust. This is his command given by himself, when he appeared to me in spirit-form last night; and how can I discard the holy injunction, confirmed as it has just been by the voices of the heavenly host? I dare no longer hesitate. I feel his spirit speaking through me; his mantle has fallen on me. O that it may also fall on you! Hear me, my friends. We live; we cannot die; we but cast off the old garment of earth, never more to be put on, and clothed anew, we enter into another and a better sphere of life, in which we will not only rejoin our dear friends who have passed from our sight, but we shall meet with our beloved teacher and guide—with Socrates, Solon, Plato, and the wise and good of all the ages and of all nations, who have been faithful in the use of the talents committed to their trust. These men hid not the truth, but proclaimed that which they knew. Let us, also, go out to the world, and preach love to our fellows—love to all mankind, as the truth of God; that there is a life surpassing this mortal life beyond death, and that that life shall have no end. I have spoken unto you the words which I received from our aged father and guide. May we meet him and all the good and wise in the great temple, where all shall mingle in holy communion of light and love.

After the burial, we retired to the temple, there to fast and pray; and that night, in solemn conclave, we resolved that henceforth our efforts would be put forth to raise up Thebes from her debased state—and that a lamp should be lit up within her that would in due time give light to all around. The prospect of ultimately delivering the nations from the prevailing darkness of ignorance and idolatry was all the more promising, inasmuch as we knew that there was one growing up (Jesus) who would yet become the great deliverer of the nations; and that, in Persia, the chief of the Magi was also on our side.

We broke off from the old and worn-out and corrupt system to which we had been attached by many a tie, and formed ourselves into a new school of theology. So it was that we went out to our fellow-men with the message as Issha had commanded. The true worship, he had said, was not confined to temples made with mortal hands, but it might be seen wherever an honest soul breathed out a prayer, whether under the broad and beautiful canopy of the sky, or in the humble dwelling of the poor. He told me that, beginning amongst my countrymen, I should go forth unto other nations, and proclaim freely all that I had received concerning man's immorality—the life of the spirit beyond the river, and the relation in which man stood towards God and his fellow-man. (You must remember that, at the time of which I am speaking, Jesus had not yet begun his great work in the neighbouring country of Judea, and we knew not of some of the great doctrines that he afterwards taught: so that I was only under the spiritual guidance of my deceased master). 'No longer,' said he, 'must you bow down before the idols of Egypt, nor do homage to the great God behind the veil, for has He not been revealed in all His glory of light and love? And as the bright beams of the sun warm the Earth, so will the knowledge of God's love open the hearts of man to the truth.'

At that time morality was at a low ebb amongst the higher class of Egyptians, and he showed me that, on this account, my mission must extend to them as well as to the poor, ignorant, and degraded son of toil. I was to lift up my voice against oppression, and denounce the robbery and tyranny that prevailed, urging them to set free their slaves from the galling chain, and no longer keep them grinding at the wheel, inasmuch as they were all the children of the same father: high and low, rich and poor, learned and ignorant, they were all the offspring of the great spirit: and that, by doing so, they would not only be doing that which was right in itself and in the sight of heaven, but they would find that, in treating their slaves as men, they would have better, more trustworthy servants.

Now for me, a single man, to undertake this mission, to go out to the people of Egypt and proclaim such doctrines, was a task of some difficulty, even confining my attention to the ignorant and degraded of the land; but to utter these truths in the hearing of the higher classes was to bring on me their bitter wrath. I was not afraid, however, of the consequences, and I felt eager to begin the work. Well I knew that, though left alone without a roof to shelter me, the great father would protect me from ill, and, if need be, shelter me even under the trees of his own beautiful creation, and as He had fed the Hebrew prophet by the ministry of the ravens of the desert, even so would he provide for me.

Conscious of the spirit-presence to aid me in my effort to do that which I deemed my duty, I feared nothing, but went forth and spoke as I was commanded. I went up even to him who was the ruler of our nation spiritually and temporally, and told him with all boldness, that the time had come for the deliverance of the people from ignorance and slavery. Why should he, the sovereign ruler of Egypt, and the religious guide of the people, sit unconcerned while those committed to his charge by the God of heaven groaned under oppression? Break asunder (I said) the bonds of the enslaved and let them go free—free as God had made them! That was enough. I might as well have appealed to the flinty rock. My mouth was stopped.

'Darest THOU a priest, thus speak to ME—me, thy prince and head?' Then turning to his attendants, he said—'Seize him, and bind him fast'. I was quickly bound, and in tones of contempt, he exclaimed, 'And who art thou that interferest with the government of the land? Why shouldst thou not be as the rest?'

'Be as the rest!' I cried, 'to cheat, to lie, to rob and wink at the deeds of the tyrant robbers, to snatch the last bite from the mouths of hungry orphans—to greedily grind the people to the dust? Rather choose I to be entombed in your foulest dungeon. There I know I shall hale higher company about me, than were I elevated to an earthly throne. Do your worst! God will protect me.'

Bound hand and foot with heavy chains, I was cast into a loathsome dungeon. But nothing of all this could bend my will, nor break my spirit. For even in that dark and loathsome prison house, I could hold sweet intercourse with the messengers of heaven. I repined not, neither raved I as a madman over my lot, but, bending low, I prayed to the great and good spirit, the creator and sustainer of all, to send His holy messengers from His throne in the heavens, to be near me, and to bear me up.

While thus I prayed on the cold floor of the dungeon, the massive building was rent asunder, and looking up in amazement at the shock, I beheld the silver moon sailing aloft over the blue and star-spangled vault of heaven. As thus I looked, there descended a flood of light so dazzlingly bright and glorious as at once made me close my natural eyes; but my inner eye was open, and I saw hundreds of angels around me. It seemed as if the whole assembly were there to give me consolation, while one of them unloosed my cruel bonds. Then I felt borne away, and when I opened my eyes, I found myself alone in a desert place. Searching for and finding my seven companions, we at length resolved to depart from Egypt, and undertake that journey we had oftentimes pondered over—a visit to Judea, where we knew we would meet with him on whom I had been taught to look upon as the heaven-sent deliverer of the nations. We felt deeply sad to leave the land of our birth, but we could not do otherwise. Our doctrines were rejected by the Egyptians, who were determined to do as their fathers had done—to die in the idolatrous slough which blinded their eyes to the glorious truth.

We required little preparation for the journey, for beyond the well-worn cloaks on our backs, the sandals on our feet, and the staffs in our hands, possessions we had none. Indeed, so ill provided were we that we had to beg our daily bread. Many of those we solicited spurned us from them. We began to feel the effect of lifting our voices against prevailing evils. Here were men, some of whom at one time would have bent the knee before me in reverence, now shunning me. And why? Because I had denounced that religious system whose priests were robbers, hoodwinking the ignorant people, and, while professing to enlighten, keeping them in the dark. They also kept back the truth that the high and holy one was not confined to mighty temples carved of stone, but might be worshipped at all times and in every place—in the verdant fields or on the mountain-tips.

Travelling onwards, we at length crossed over by the head of the Red Sea: not as the ancient Hebrews, bent on slaughter of their enemies, the tribes whose territories they invaded. No, our mission was of a very different nature; we went forth to do battle with the evil in the hearts of men: to drive out man's great enemy—sin; to show the path which would lead them from darkness to light, and usher in the happy time—that time, pictured by the poets of Greece, when the Seraphim walked and talked with men, till pride crept in, and they foolishly imagined themselves equal to the gods.

In our wanderings through some of the wild tracts, we met with one here and there in possession of the true light, and on reaching the mountainous parts, we found some men who had embraced the truth spiritually given to them, and who valued the privilege of communion with the spirit world. With them we resolved to abide for a time. We learned that they were exiles—driven there because of their faith.

In one of these retreats, we found two or three Syrian brethren living together. They had laboured hard and suffered much in the service of truth, and had committed their experiences to writing, that when called away from Earth, some memorials of their work should remain for the use of others. We found too, that they knew of Jesus and his mission in Judea. They had been told by spirit messengers of his wonderful birth, and of the great work he was destined to accomplish. And when we told them our story, and that we were on our way to join ourselves to him, they joyfully embraced us, exclaiming, 'Thanks be to God, now we have some to sympathise with us.' Accordingly, they resolved to accompany us, and enlist also in the service of the great prince, the light of the world.

We rested with the brethren for a short time, as we were footsore and weary in body, and discouraged in spirit. For some time our only shelter at night from the heavy dew had been the outspread branches of a tree; for in some places we encountered the bitter opposition of those who, though making the loudest professions of religion, would listen to no new doctrine, but, stirring the people up against us, drove us out into the wilds. But when our spirits got low, the words were sweetly whispered in our ears, 'Rise, my sons, go forth on your mission; be not discouraged—ye shall triumph in the end; and heaven's brightest diadems shall be yours.' These gracious words revived our drooping spirits.

At length we resumed our journey, our band reinforced by the three of the brethren we had met with. We travelled on till we reached the district of country where the cities of Moab had flourished in the olden time. At this time, many of them were in ruins or fast falling into decay. It is a sad sight to look on a wasted country. O war, cruel, pitiless war! How often hast thou swept away innocent with the guilty, sparing neither age nor sex in thy ruthless, reckless course! How often hath thy sackings and slaughter laid the fair city desolate, while the cries of the wretched inhabitants were choked 'mid the smoke and flames of their burning dwellings! The doctrines of Jesus put into practice would put an end to all that.

Having travelled on through Moab, doing what we could by the way, we at length entered Palestine, in which at that time were a number of fair cities and towns. These were under the Roman rule, and when we came to know the character of the inhabitants, we considered it was well that they were under the Roman government. We had on our journey met with wild and barbarous men, but nothing to be compared with many of these Judean cities. It was not safe even to walk along their streets; for murders, assassinations, and robberies were constantly occurring. Compared with neighbouring nations, they were vile indeed. When our eyes witnessed the prevailing iniquity, we no longer wondered that the great deliverer was sent to them.

They proudly asserted that they were the chosen of the most high—and doubtless, when we looked to the history of the surrounding nations, God had dealt wonderfully with them; and yet with the consciousness of this, these men thought nothing of engaging in the solemn service of God in the temple, and, on leaving it, embruing their hands in the blood of their neighbours. God had dealt with them as he had dealt with no others, according to their own records, yet they would take no lesson. His goodness and his severity had alike been without effect on the rebellious, erring children of Israel. And now he sends his son to them, the murder of whom will be the greatest of their crimes.

We Egyptians have been described by the Hebrews in their holy books as gross idolators, slaveholders, and hard taskmasters. Doubtless these early Egyptians, like their neighbouring nations, enslaved their prisoners of war. The Hebrews had come among us, as shepherds, seeking food for themselves and their flocks, and because one of their race, whom. they had years before sold into slavery, who had done good service to Egypt and had become a great ruler, they were welcomed, and had the fairest portion of the land given to them as a possession. Famine had spread over all the nations, and many were fed by Egypt out of the abundant stores collected through the foresight of the youthful Hebrew ruler, who appears to have been favoured by God to foresee the coming scarcity, even when there were no signs of such to be seen—storing up corn in houses all over the land in seasons of plenty: thus making the Egyptians the masters of the famine-stricken nations around, who were dependent on them for bread.

The father of this Hebrew youth had been highly honoured by Pharaoh, and, as I have said, got a present from him of the best land, on which he and his children lived; and for generations the Hebrews prospered greatly in Egypt, becoming numerous and strong. But as they grew in strength, they also grew in pride, and made themselves disagreeable to the Egyptians, grumbling against the nation which had sheltered and nourished them; and, to obtain the mastery, these Hebrews at length threatened to crush the Egyptians, but were crushed themselves, and compelled to labour for the support they claimed; for these idle grumblers would do nothing—they wanted to live on the toil of others. Man was made to work, not to stand still.

Moses, as I have said, was brought up and educated as a prince, and revelled in all the luxury of the Egyptian court; but he was also (secretly) a priest, thoroughly initiated into all the mysteries of the temple service. There should certainly be no mysteries connected with the worship of God; but in these temple communities there was much more taught than belonged to mere worship, even in my day; and my eyes were opened to see the evils that prevailed, and I denounced them.

The secrets of the priests consisted in a knowledge of chemistry and other arts by practising which before the eyes of the ignorant they were led to think that the priests were something more than men. As a consequence, these deceivers had no difficulty in filling their pockets at the expense of the deluded people; and Moses was no exception to the rule, even though he was a prince of the house of Pharaoh, who was also the head of the priesthood.

But Moses, according to our records, slew a man, and fled from Egypt—from all the glory and grandeur of the Egyptian court, and became the humble shepherd of the flocks of a Median priest. He afterwards married the priest's daughter, and settled down as a shepherd far many years. At last he appeared in Egypt as the chosen leader of the Hebrews to deliver them from the bondage of their masters. I have no right to question the position he assumed. For their great forefather Abraham, who was respected by the Egyptians of his day, prophesied that his descendants should possess the land of Canaan; and the efforts which Moses put forth for the rescue of his nation from bondage under the direction of heaven.

It was well known to some that one of our shepherd kings, living at the same time as the great Hebrew patriarch, after building one of the pyramids, conceived the idea of setting up a kingdom in Canaan, and in course of time he erected a city which he named Salem, where he ruled as king and priest. The nations around him however, combined to drive him back to Egypt; but Abraham, coming to know that this king, with whom he was on terms of friendship, was hard beset by his foes, came to the rescue, and valorously dispersed the assailants. Melchisedek there and then made a solemn covenant with Abraham that Salem should become the inheritance of his descendants. This shepherd king of Egypt was a true worshipper of God, having broken off from the mysteries of the Egyptians, and entertained doctrines similar to those taught by the Persians.

Now, this promise made to Abraham was handed down from generation to generation, and no doubt Moses and the chief men amongst the Hebrews were aware of it, and claimed the promise as coming from God. Whether they were right in so doing, I cannot tell. This much I can say, that of all the plagues and judgements given in the Hebrew books as falling on the Egyptians, I do not find the slightest trace in the historical records of Egypt.

The Hebrews left Egypt carrying off with them an immense spoil, which, according to their own account, they had obtained by fraud from the people of Egypt. They robbed all around them on the pretence of borrowing—not sparing the poor of the land; a cruel, heartless act this, but quite in harmony with their general character. These men scrupled not at falsehood to obtain their neighbours' property, and would have others believe that they had the command of God for the dastardly deed. Does God permit lies? Does he sanction fraud? The Hebrews have a grand tale about the anxiety of the Egyptians to bring back the fugitives; but the expedition of Pharaoh was not for the purpose of getting back the Hebrews, but to recover the property they had stolen away. The ruler could not see his people robbed—even of the very arms they carried—and not put forth a hand to restore them. Hebrew writers say that they had a right to take all they could, for they had toiled for it. Admitting this, why should they also rob the poor of the land?

Well, they followed their leader's directions, and they got into a strange position. Had I been their leader, I certainly would have chosen a very different route. They found themselves hemmed in by natural barriers on both sides with the sea before them. Fortunately for them, there had just been an earthquake or convulsion in the neighbourhood, and the Red Sea had been subjected to subsequent upheavings, and that portion of it which they had reached they found dry; in their extremity, with the Egyptians following on their rear, they crossed over; but the tidal wave came back to its original bed, sweeping away the mighty hosts of Egypt's warriors, and also the tail of the Hebrews. Their own writers forget to give this tail-piece, but such is according to Egyptian records.

Having wandered from the subject of the journey my brethren and I were making to Judea, I must return to it. During our travels we became aware that we had come into possession of various spiritual gifts—in particular, the power of healing. Each of us was endowed, but not all alike. I myself had the gift of tongues. Accordingly, as we journeyed on, we were not neglectful of the power so freely bestowed upon on, and whenever we got the opportunity, endeavoured to do all the good we could. It was while thus engaged one day, we first met some of the personal followers of Jesus. They were some of those who had been sent out by him, commissioned to proclaim the truth, and to heal the sick. They found us doing the same work as themselves, and they wondered: yet we did it under the direction of the same spirit. But they turned away from us, evidently despising us because of our mean and miserable appearance, for we were wayworn, our clothing ragged and torn, and our feet, which at one time had sandals, were now, by reason of the long journey, cut, bruised, and bare. Truly we were in a wretched condition, and because of this, they evidently carried back with them an evil impression of our work to Jesus. But we went on with the good work, hundreds gathering around us wherever we went. We spoke as we were led by the spirit; the words were not ours, and many received the truths which we proclaimed.

At length we met him whom we had travelled so far to see. We found him in the neighbourhood of Bethlehem, where my venerable friend the Persian had welcomed his advent to Earth. On coming near to him, he looked at us, and turning to his disciples, he said, 'These are men who have come from Egypt, and who have been taught by the spirit of truth.' Then turning to us, he saluted and welcomed us gladly. I will never forget during the ages of eternity the gracious welcome we received from Jesus our loving prince.

3

The Baptist, Herod, and the state of the Jewish nation

Before entering further in my narrative, I must once more say something on that which I have already alluded to—I mean the character of the people of Judea about the time of our visit. They had long been a by-word amongst the nations for depravity. Of course, I do not mean to say that there were no good men amongst them; for there were some of these, and very many, who, throughout their history as a nation, had shone as the stars. At this time however, the Jews seemed to have reached the lowest depth of social disorganisation—so much so that no one could be said to be sure of his life in the streets, even in Jerusalem, the holy city. Terror reigned, and each one distrusted his neighbour. One might be walking quietly and peaceably on his way, and, ere he reached his home, the dagger of the assassin ended his earthly career. And these murderous deeds were not confined to the streets and lanes of the city. Many were afraid to sit down to meat in their own houses, lest they should become the victims of the secret poisoner. Crime was rampant; the religious sects entertained the bitterest hatred to all who differed from themselves; and turmoil from the king to the peasant, prevailed all over the community.

It was to such action the prophet and reformer John the Baptist had been raised up, sometime before our visit. John, as you may be aware, was nearly related to Jesus, their mothers being cousins. John was the son of a priest, and from his infancy was fully endowed with the spirit. There had always been something eccentric about him; for even when a boy, instruction by the ordinary methods was lost upon him, and what he did acquire was ascribed to an inner teaching. In this he was unlike Jesus, for he, when a boy, was an apt scholar in any branch of study. Of John it may be truly said, he was the pioneer of Jesus. Indeed he was destined for that work; for, from his boyhood till he was cut off in the prime of manhood, he preached to the people, in his wild but honest way, the grand truths which the lord was afterwards to elaborate and enforce. Many of those who had listened to the burning language of John, as he denounced the sensuality and the hypocrisy of the time, thought he was under the control of a spirit. For some time he refused to wear ordinary clothing, and clad himself instead in the skins of animals; living on herbs, and quenching his thirst by water from the wayside stream. Notwithstanding these peculiarities, John effected a great and good work in Judea, for many of the people of all classes were deeply impressed by the truths he so boldly uttered, and were baptised by him; and even some of the rough soldiers became disciples of the Baptist. Honour and praise be unto him; for, as a great reformer and a fearless prophet of God, he was indeed worthy of all honour. Nor was his power felt only by the people. Herod the tetrarch was not ashamed of the company of this wild preacher of the wilderness, but esteemed him greatly—for a time, at least.

I have said that Judea was at that time a scene of turmoil and murderous deeds; and this may readily be believed when the character of Herod, their ruler, is considered. He had cast lustful eyes on his bother's wife, who infamously deserted her husband—Herod marrying her after his own wife had fled to her father. The incestuous pair were evidently ill at ease. They could not bear the sight of the man they had so foully injured, and, it was said, got him put out of their way in course of time by slow poison. But the Baptist, having boldly denounced their unlawful connection, was thrown into prison. This did not, however, satisfy the guilty paramour of Herod, for, while inflamed with wine, she induced him to give her an order for the murder of John, which was speedily executed. The miserable man, who regretted deeply the result of his drunkenness, never afterwards prospered, but was at length degraded from his kingly office, and banished by the Roman government;

while his wretched partner fled as a fugitive into distant Spain. When such were the acts done in the place of the ruler, what might be expected in the dens and hovels of the people?

The wickedness of these Hebrews, I repeat, exceeded that of any other nation. They were a foul blot of the face of God's fair Earth. When I thought of it, my soul was filled with loathing and detestation of their atrocities.

And this was the condition of the people to whom the one man was sent. The great work lay all before him—to lift them up, out of the deep, dark pit into which they had fallen, to the light of truth and love. But alas! they who should have welcomed him with open arms were blind; they knew him not. 'This man!' they cried. 'This man, Jesus, the son of a carpenter, with his ignorant, uneducated fishermen, what can he do?' And he, the prince of light, to come to such a people! How many of the surrounding nations would have honoured him—would have prized him as a gift from heaven! But that would not have suited him. He sought for no trumpet to sound his praise. Ever calm, wise, and humble in all he did and said, he lifted not up his voice in the streets, but, in loving accents, spoke plainly to the people concerning the inner truth of their own religious system—the great truth which had been crusted over by the lying traditions of ages, buried out of sight by the cunning craft of priests—the truth which, when believed, would make them free: that all men were brethren, children of the same father; and that His loving-kindness embraced the whole human race. Glory and honour for ever be unto him, that he shrank not back from the great work of man's redemption from the slavery in which he lay bound!

At this time the Jews generally might be classed under three religious parties or sects—the Pharisees, Sadducees, and Essenes. The Pharisee was known by his strict attention to outward acts of worship, setting himself up as holy, and far beyond his neighbours of other sects, because of his conformity to rites and ceremonies, and his long and oft-repeated prayers.

He was distinguished from other mortals, as we walked along, by the gravity of his countenance, and the upturning of his eyes towards heaven. He was holy in his own eyes at least.

The Essenes were men of a very different stamp. From this class came the followers of the Lord Jesus—being in a manner ready to follow him, because of their similarity to him in doctrine and practice. They were strict in their lives: simple in their habits, eating of the plainest food, drinking no strong drinks, and washing their bodies twice a day, in the cool of the morning and evening. By a strict adherence to this course, many of them lived to a good old age. Their clothing too, was of the simplest description, inasmuch as all they possessed they carried on their backs. None was richer, none was poorer than another. They ate and drank alike, and they were sheltered alike. The children born to them were all equally cared for by the community. Some of these Essenes, like the devout Persians, rose at daybreak and engaged in prayer. On entering a city, they claimed and found shelter from their brethren resident therein. And so, when Jesus and his disciples came into a strange city, it was the poor Essenes of the place who opened their doors to him—not the rich Pharisees, nor the sneering Sadducees.

Shortly after the master had begun his work, he selected twelve of his followers to be near his person, and accompany him from place to place. In walking by the wayside, in the streets, and even when they sat to eat, he was continually instructing the twelve and the other disciples, so that they might be able to do the same for others. Though I did not reckon myself equal with those favoured ones whom my lord had chosen to be near him, so that they might be instructed as his messengers to spread abroad doctrines, yet was I always ready to do what I could; and I had a good opportunity granted to me, inasmuch as there were some of my own countrymen, exiled from Egypt, settled in Judea. This was my field of labour, and in speaking to them, I felt I could strike home. Nor were my efforts unsuccessful, for some of them became true followers of Jesus.

The Temple of Jerusalem at the time I am speaking of, had had been finished but a short time before, and the vast building was truly a beautiful sight for the eye to rest on. It had been set up for the worship of the most high; but through the cupidity of the priests the great house of prayer had become, at the time of our visit, terribly desecrated. When our little company entered within its walls, we found its porches, not thronged by devout worshippers, but by persons buying and selling. It had become an exchange—a common market-place. The first time I saw a frown of anger on the face of Jesus was then. He cast a glance of wrathful indignation on the scene, then drawing a cord from his waist, he twisted it into a lash, and with the arm of a giant and the denunciation of a god, he drove out the mercenary herd, while none dared to withstand him, but fled in utter dismay. The temple of the living God, dedicated to solemn worship, turned by the connivance of greedy priests, into a market-place! No wonder that the master, in righteous anger, drove out with a scourge the profaners of the holy place.

After this many of the Hebrews in Jerusalem, of high and low degree, became followers of Jesus—some of them secretly; but there were others who were not afraid to speak openly of him, notwithstanding the hostility of both the high priest and Herod, who wished to crush him. But the master was unmoved, quietly saying to those of us who were around him, 'Be ye not afraid. My time is not yet come. The work I am sent to do must be finished, and then the time will come when I shall be delivered into their hands.' But we did not then consider fully the meaning of his words. We thought only how best to gather in adherents, so as to have strength to withstand those who were opposed to us. The very worst of these were the Sadducees—most abominable sect. The Pharisees—though many of them were thorough hypocrites—had at least a form of piety; but these Sadducees were utterly detestable. Why, they were not even civil to the members of their own households. They had no belief in a future life—their only care seemed to be for themselves, regardless of the welfare of others. Many a bitter scoff they hurled at us—even raising false and malicious charges against us. But what cared we for all they could say! Having the lord of truth on our side we were strong.

I often wondered at the craftiness of the Pharisees and Sadducees, who seemed to think that all learning and wisdom was confined to their own little circle—how cunningly they would put their ensnaring question to a single man, so that they might catch him tripping, and enable them to have something laid to his charge. They thought he was ignorant! They knew not—these tricksters never dreamt that the simple Nazarene, round whom they gathered, had been educated not only in Persia, Egypt and Greece, but in India and the East. But notwithstanding their mean and spiteful opposition, he wearied not in his gracious work, but at all times and wherever he went, wondrous good was done by him to the souls and bodies of the distressed; and not only so, his ears were open to the cry of the poor and desolate ones; and when his keen but pitying eye caught sight of the helpless widow and orphan, he would turn to the purse-bearer of the band, and bid him put his hand into the empty bag, and give them a coin he found there that they might buy food.

In a short time the fame of Jesus was widely spread amongst the people in Jerusalem and the neighbourhood; and the number of followers gathering around him and accompanying him wherever he went being nearly a thousand persons, it was clearly seen that something needed to be done in order to carry out the work efficiently. Accordingly the master went out from Jerusalem, followed only by the twelve and some others. We visited various places, in furtherance of the great object to which we had devoted ourselves. After going from town to town on the shores of the sea, our master resolved to send out some of those not numbered amongst the twelve, on a mission to various places outside Judea: some to Rome and Greece; while I and two others of my own company were chosen by him to go to a town in the close neighbourhood of Alexandria, in which place a number of devout Hebrews, exiles from Judea, had gathered together, and erected a synagogue for the worship of God. To these we were to proclaim the truth we had received; telling them all that we had seen, and heard, and that he whom they had been long waiting for—the Messiah—had come.

The night before parting, we gathered round the supper table somewhat sorrowful. We felt that with Jesus beside us we were strong; without him, weak. But he seeing our sadness of face, spoke wisely and lovingly to us. He told us not to be disheartened; that though plunged into adversity, made the butt of the scoffer, and denounced as madmen, we had truth and heaven on our side. Turning to me and my two companions, he said, 'Show unto my countrymen in Egypt, who have been driven away because of their faith in the promised one, that the Messiah has come, and that it is even he that sent you unto them. Be witnesses for me of all you have seen and heard; and preach to them the great doctrines—love: to do to others that which they would have others do to them. Tell them I love them; I love you; I love all.'

After supper, the last we should take with him for some time, he rose up, and we who were to go away, bent before him. Then, with uplifted hands, he blessed us, asking the father who had sent him, to open up our path and strengthen us for the work we had to do. Raising his eyes to heaven, He prayed: 'O glorious and mighty father, great spirit of all, creator of the worlds, look graciously on these my brethren whom I now send forth into the world. O Father, may they know and feel that all strength is to be found in Thee: and that in themselves there is no strength. Give unto them, therefore, that which they lack, that they may be able to declare Thy truth, even unto those who seek their lives, that Thou art indeed their father and their friend, waiting for their return unto Thee. Great God of truth, may these messengers of Thy truth, sent out to the scattered of Israel, and to the people of the Gentiles, know assuredly that Thou art with them always, and that Thou wilt guide them in the right way, and protect them from all the devices of the wicked.'

After lovingly embracing those who were about to leave, he turned to me and said, 'And thou, companion of my youth; thou who didst share with me the fatherly care and instruction of the good old Issha, I send thee back to thy people and to my people to declare what thou hast seen of me. Go forth, my brother, strong in the conviction, that God is with thee. I know that thou wilt prosper in the good work set before thee. The holy one in whose services thou art engaged will bless thee; and he who was father and guide to us when we were boys will, in spirit, still direct thee in thy steps. Look well to thy brethren whom I send with thee. The journey you undertake is beset with dangers from beasts of prey and men more savage than the beasts. But be not afraid, my brethren, God will shield you from all evil. Beloved, farewell till we meet again. The time will not be long.'

After supping with Jesus and the disciples, we retired to rest, and early the following morning, with our well-worn cloaks wrapped round us and staff in hand, we set out on our journey.

4

Mission to Egypt. A vision of past and future

The route we took for our return to Egypt was different from that taken when we had left to find the master. Now we went toward the Jordan, and followed its course southward till we reached the Dead Sea, on the western shores of which we continued our journey. It was not the easiest route, but we selected it because we might have the opportunity of speaking with the inhabitants of a number of villages in that obscure part of the country.

In one of these sequested villages we met with a small community that were neither Hebrews, nor even belonging to any of the nations surrounding Judea. They appeared to me to be a mixture of races. After some intercourse with them, we found them the most intelligent people, perhaps, that ever we had met with. We began, as was our wont, to speak to them concerning the new light which had sprung up, talking for some time of our master, and his wonderful words and works, when they calmly told us that they knew all about the recorded predictions concerning the great deliverer; that they, a small band of men and women, had been drawn to that secluded spot, bound together by the oneness of faith in the coming one; and that they had been blessed and greatly strengthened in their faith by revelations of the spirit world through dreams and visions. We then gave them the farthest information concerning our master, his character and his mission; and also told them about the great and gracious acts he had done for the relief of those who were suffering in body and in mind. They expressed their gratification with the good news we had brought them, believing that he whose character we had described was, in truth, the one whose appearance they had been waiting, and glad were they to know that he was so very near to them. They were greatly interested also in our account of the wonderful cures effected by Jesus, for they themselves were gifted with similar healing powers; but, though believing them to be derived from the same source, they acknowledged they were much less in degree. Such as they were however, they had put forth for the relief of the sick and those who were otherwise disabled.

We tarried for a time with this blessed community, which only numbered a score or two; and while with them we were privileged to listen to an address given by an aged man, one of their number, I cannot describe it otherwise than as truly wonderful. Our parting from the little company was very tender; for in all our experience we had never met with people so congenial—so warm-hearted, as these were. Indeed, they seemed to me as angelic beings, encased in mortal frames—men and women really possessed by great and good and holy spirits who had left the earth ages before. We would have liked a longer stay amongst these good people, to listen to some of their inspired ones, discoursing of the early times of the world; but we knew that our master's work must not be neglected—so we went our way.

After a long and weary march through the wilderness under a burning sun, we came to a halt about the close of day. Our lips and throats were parched, for good water was scarce in that desert region; while the noxious fumes of sulphur and salt from the lake added to our wretchedness. Our provisions were also short. But, in our extremity, we remembered the words of Jesus: 'Heed ye not when want comes upon you: ye shall be fed.' We knew that the very birds of the air would, if need be, bring us food, and that among even the dry rocks of the wilderness we should find springs of water. We had faith in his word.

The great sun at length went down, and night coming on, we lay down to rest on the bare ground, exposed to the heavy dews; with no curtains over us save the over-arching canopy of the heavens, draped with starry jewels, while the moon shed a silvery radiance over the lake and its rock-bound shore. With a stone which we had selected as a pillow, and our cloaks wrapped well about us, we felt as happy as the mightiest princes of the earth stretched on their soft and gorgeous beds. Aye, and much more so; for we lay down with clear consciences—our hearts open to God, to whom with bared heads and on bended knees we had commended ourselves, praying for the protection of His holy ones. There was nothing to be feared from man or beast, and our sleep was calm and unruffled, while nature refreshed our weary joints.

And while thus we slept we became witnesses of a vision. Whether a dream or a vision it matters not, but each of us felt as if we had lived in a far back age, before the earth was brought forth. A great panorama moved, as it were, before our eyes, the scenes depicted on which were composed of all things that had transpired from the beginning of time down and down in the world's history to our own day, and beyond it.

First as we looked, we saw three thrones. The largest of the three, in the centre, was gloriously bright as if the light of ten thousand suns was thrown in upon it. There was no one there, not even the holiest ones could see Him who sat thereon, because of the dazzling light. On the right of that throne of light, was another throne, and on it we saw one whom we knew as our lord the prince—he whom we had just left, Jesus the Nazarene, wandering over Judea without a home to shelter him, and sharing with his poor band the little that he had. Yet there on the right of the glorious unseen one, he sat, while another high and holy one sat on the left. We ourselves seemed to form a part of the infinite host of happy and pure spirits that stood around that great centre of light, while the arches of heaven resounded with the harmonies of innumerable trumpets, all as it seemed to us, proclaiming with one voice, the greatness, the goodness, and the glory of the invisible one, now sitting in council with the myriads of his bright and holy ones, called together from the vast and glorious kingdoms of the diverse of spirit.

It was decreed, and the fiat of heaven went forth, to launch material worlds into the boundless ocean of space. Then we looked again, and we beheld the mighty ones at work amid the great forces of spirit, till one great ball was formed, round which other great bodies—new-made worlds—took up their places. We saw the foundations of the earth laid. Let us pause while we look for a little into this great and wonderful operation of the master's hand. Ah! How unlike the workings of man. Here are no quarryings for the rock—no hewing and chiselling of stone for the erection of puny structures. But the foundations of which the mighty master built his worlds were thin gaseous vapours, brought together one after another, till they became dense masses. And such was the earth.

We saw as it were the likeness of smoke from burning wood, curling and curling out till it became one vast flame; while as we looked, on and on it rolled round greater orbs that had been made before; round and round flies the huge mass of fire and vapour and smoke with incalculable speed, and while it rushes on its course it gets harder and harder. But ever onward goes this blazing ball till, hot and burning within, crusted without, it draws nearer and still nearer, with its course more regular, to its grand attracting body. On goes this now misty globe till its dense vapours become waters, and now it gets into a regular track as it courses round the sun. We looked again, and we saw in the circling ball of water life in various forms. Then from the same great council that first gave forth the fiat of creation, there came the command, let chaos bring forth land, abode of spirit! Then we saw great fountains of rocks rise out of the waters; continents and seas were formed; and as we looked, gradually the dry land appeared, formed by the tear and wear of the rocks thrown up, from the crust, above the waters, and these in turn rushed into the new-formed hollows.

Then as we looked down from our lofty position as spectators, we saw the earth clad with verdure; another look, and we saw great plants and huge animals in the waters and on the land; then stage by stage of transformation, and animals of many kinds appeared to us, while the thick haze that had hitherto covered the earth disappeared, and she smiled in gladness and in beauty.

At length we saw man take his appointed place. Spirit began the mortal life. To our view those happy mortals did not seem to be shut out from the consciousness of having been in a former and higher state of existence; they appeared to us, in our vision, to live in a close and constant communion with the spirit world—a continual ascending to and descending from it, and happiness the blessed lot of man. This was the golden age of the Grecian poets. We saw that, by natural law, men increased in number on the earth—their spiritual part supplied from on high. But though full-grown as spirits, when brought into contact with the material body they became infants—all memory of previous life was blotted out; we saw, however, that as time wore on, they began (so intimate was the communion) to have glimpses of their spirit existence. (I myself often tried to remember the time when I lived in spirit before the earth-life, but I could not; only, in this vision, I must have seen myself there).

So, in our vision, we saw, that as men multiplied and spread over the earth, gathering flocks and herds, one wandering this way, the other that, they began to come together for worship in groves, but still in communion with the spirit world, and in the enjoyment of all that flows from that communion. As time went on, we saw great and magnificent cities arise: but how unlike the workmanship of the great architect! Then we saw mankind beginning to depart from the right way. There seemed to be a gradual falling away from spirit intercourse, until, at length, there was but one here and there who were true worshippers of God. Men became proud, self-sufficient, vain. Then we saw the upsetting of laws, war, and bloodshed; and mankind, once so peaceful and happy, became ravenous as beasts of prey. We saw man against man, nation against nation, in hot religious strife, and ignorance and superstition covered the world in darkness. (Ah! Why should man depart from the simplicity of truth—from the worship of the great spirit, to whom alone all service, homage, and honour is due! He seeketh not such for His own good, but for ours. (All good things cometh from Him, and He asketh nothing in return).

Again, in our vision, we beheld a small company of true worshippers take up their abode on the banks of the Nile, where in words simple, and from the heart, but in a language not now understood, they sang hymns to the creator—the invisible God. There these simple shepherds fed their flocks and herds in peace. We saw them building those cities, the ruins of which show the wisdom and the greatness that then existed. Then came their kings—the shepherd kings of Egypt, many of them good and great men, worshippers of the one great spirit. Then we saw another dynasty of kings, and Egypt rise in glory and splendour with her Pharaohs, builders of mighty temples, but with a worship dark and mysterious.

Then we saw other nations erecting similar temples, their worship in harmony with their ignorance; while the people, blinded by false teachers, fell down in prayer to idols the work of their own hands. (Ah, why will men listen to the silly conceits of proud and selfish priests!) The golden age was swamped. Communion with the good and great of the spirit world was almost at an end. But amid the thick spiritual darkness, we saw that light sprang up here and there. Great reformers arose, and did all they could to bring back their countrymen to the truth. Some of these were successful in their efforts. We saw them in Persia and in other nations of the east. But, in general, mankind went on in their deep degradation into the lowest depths.

Then I saw myself with my aged and venerated father, the humble and holy priest. I saw the old man instructing me opening up my youthful mind to a knowledge of the symbols on Egyptian worship. All this I saw, and each one of us saw his own individual history in vision. Then I beheld my beloved teacher pass away into the world of spirits I saw myself waked up, and with burning soul, throwing to the winds all the forms of the old faith, and thinking to over turn the superstition and priestcraft of Egypt by the sweep of my single arm. Alas! all I could do was but little. I saw my journey to Judea, and the meeting with Jesus my lord and master.

The tidal wave of the religious ideas had risen in the east, and as mankind went from one quarter to another, spreading themselves over the earth, these ideas or notions were carried with them. Kings and priests entertained them—cherished them—and the people bent themselves in slavish submission to tyranny on the one hand and priestcraft on the other. The thick darkness prevailed in many a region, and the benighted people groped their way, and longed wearily for the day-break. They knew not that the light, destined to enlighten the world, had appeared in Judea—that true light which we had seen dimly beginning to rise in Egypt, in Persia, and other eastern lands; and that the great light-bringer (He whom we had seen sitting enthroned in glory) was even then wandering about with his poor followers, without a house to shelter him, and often dependent on others for daily bread. (Ah! How shall I tell you of his heart of love: how his great soul went out in deep compassion for even those who spurned him from their doors). And now, for our vision, we see him looking down upon Jerusalem, while tears of bitter grief come from those wonderful eyes, as he bemoans the condition and fate of this self-doomed city. O great God! How can I forget those tears! That sad, sad face! Ah, how often had we seen him thus! Seldom he smiled: he seemed at all times as one ready to give up everything—life itself—for his fellow-men. Where, O where, over all earth's history, can you find one to compare with Jesus?

We saw the results of our mission to Egypt, and the dangers and difficulties I encountered on my return journey to Judea. We then saw our lord and master dragged by the wicked hands of his own countrymen and accused unjustly before a foreign judge—when even that Roman would have spared him, but for the turbulence and threatenings of the infuriated priests, who howled like wolves for the life-blood of him we loved so well. We saw the shameful death on Calvary. We saw the assembly of the followers of Jesus after the crucifixion and resurrection—no, not resurrection, for he was not dead. The spirit of our master left the body behind, and entered Hades to lead forth in triumph many of those who had been bound in darkness. Even amid the gloom of the dark regions light began to break in. The scene was changed, and we saw that assembly broken up by fierce persecution, and the faithful followers of Jesus scattered abroad. We saw next the beautiful city of Jerusalem laid low—ravaged and made waste by the iron bands of the besiegers. We saw how those who had been driven out by persecution worked and strove even unto death on behalf of the truth. And then we witnessed the aged Hafed, whose past career we had also seen—the prince Arch-Magus of Persia—condemned to die. We saw his martyrdom. Then followed one after another, martyrs to the truth gladly meeting death in diverse shapes for the sake of Jesus our lord. All this we saw—even my own death; but I saw not the manner of that death. Of that I shall yet require to speak.

Again the scene was changed. We perceived the true light borne into many lands by the humble followers of Jesus—men who had nothing of the learning of Egypt, Persia, or Greece. They went forth strong in the faith of their master, and with the power of his spirit. Then, as we looked, we saw Rome, the mistress of the world—Rome, which had subdued the nations to her sway from Gaul on the west to India on the east—trampling under her iron hooves all that stood in her way—we saw even this powerful nation, all-conquering, imperial Rome, accepting these truths. Next came the utter desolation of the once-famous Egypt and her great and marvellous buildings, while other countries, celebrated in history, became, by the violence of men, barren and wasted as the desert.

Another change, and we saw great Rome herself, which had given laws to the peoples east and west, north and south, crushed and bleeding beneath the feet of northern hosts. Still further, we saw the western nations become Christians, and blessed and made happy by the change. Time rolls on; again the dark clouds gather, and the light is once more quenched; liberty is groaning under the fetters of tyrants; ignorance prevails, and the people sink into idolatry; priestcraft is at her old work; falsehood is honoured and glorified, while truth is despised—crucified the laws of the prince are, even by those who bear his name, trampled beneath their feet.

Again, there came another scene before us, and we witnessed the truth spreading widely; but as it branched out amongst the nations of the west, we saw many eager to mix up their own ideas with the simple doctrines of Jesus, thus hiding from the people the truths which he had made free to all. (When he spoke to the thousands of Judea, did he not speak so that a child could understand him? He would not have his light put under a bushel. Ah, no; he ever spoke simply, clearly; and, though in parables at times, these were well understood by the people who listened to him). Then, as our vision continued, we saw those men, priests, who professed to be the divinely-appointed guardians of the truth, selling that truth, as they have ever done, for the world's money, and honour and power. (They went not out as we had done, with our cloaks round us, our feet unshod, and knowing not where to find our next meal. No, these false priests cared nothing for the people; they robbed them of their goods, in order that they themselves might revel in sensuality and sloth).

But while we continued to look, we beheld in the darkness a bright little spark burning. (It has ever been thus in all the ages of the past: the true light is never altogether quenched. Some humble one, none of the earth's great men—it may be a simple peasant—is the heaven-sent bearer of that light that shall in due time burst out into a mighty flame to enlighten mankind). We saw that light begin to burn, even in this your day. (Our friend Hafed has already told you of one who, so far as we can see, is near at hand—one destined to crush down the materialism of your time, which is more deadly now than ever before—worse than that of Greece or Rome). And this great reformer, or messenger, was endowed with powers, enabling him to overthrow the barriers that were lying in the way of the world's happiness—to open up the spirit world to man—and to lead and guide mankind in spiritual wisdom and knowledge.

We saw, but past your day, the long-desired, the long-promised return of that glorious time, the theme of prophets and poets of the long past—the golden age of the Greeks, the paradise of the Hebrews, when man served God in truth, drinking in heaven's wisdom, and communing with angels even as he would with his fellows. We saw barrier after barrier removed by the mighty power of the great reformer. We saw others with the same power following him—one after another overthrowing the iniquitous systems of the world which had long hindered man's highest good. We saw these great messengers of the prince triumphant; and then we beheld ushered in the blessed age so long prayed for, when the prince of peace has his throne in the hearts of men: when each vies in goodness and truth with his neighbour, when deceit and wickedness no longer prevail, and every man reads his bother's mind as he does his own.

5

A return to Judea and Jesus

The wonderful vision of which I have given you an account passed away; and the sun began to break out on the eastern sky as we lifted our heads from our stony pillow. Gradually he rose in beauty and strength, and much I loved to look on the bright luminary, as a glorious emblem of the great father, who pours down continually His light and life on all His works. Remembering the lessons taught me by Hafed of this great symbol of worship, we reverently bent our knees in prayer, and raised our voices to the mighty God, the source of all light and love, thanking Him for the gracious revelation which had been made to us. What were we that we should be chosen to see these things? Thousands of our fellow-men were more deserving than we were. But, in all this there was a purpose, and that was, to impress on us, who were sent out to the world by our prince, the relation in which he, the son of earth, stood to the great father in the highest heavens. In our sojourn with him we had seen him humbly sharing with his followers daily bread; but in vision our eyes had seen him at the right hand of the invisible God.

Before we started on our journey, like the patriarchs of the olden time, we raised a monument of stones on the spot where our eyes had been blessed: so that if ever we came back that way, we would again raise our voices in thanksgiving to Him who had so graciously dealt with us there.

At length we went on our way, rejoicing with each other as we walked along over all that had been revealed to us. On our journey we lost no opportunity of imparting to others the knowledge of all we had received from the master, and of that also which we had seen in vision. We tried to speak to the people in the simplest language, so that they might clearly understand us. By doing so, and boldly pointing out that which we considered wrong in their lives, we succeeded in drawing many away from their lusts to a course of purity and truth.

To you, spiritualists of the present day, I would say, Be not afraid to declare to your fellow-men all that ye have received from the spirit world. But, take heed—listen *NOT* to communications of evil: see that that which is given to you is consistent with righteousness and truth as seen in the character of the master. Bring your communications to the bar of reason; and if found wanting, then thrust them aside as worthless—evil. When, however, you do find in them lessons of truth and goodness, retain them, prize them, and fear not to show them to all around. In this as in all other things be guided by the example of Jesus. He withheld not the truths from his countrymen, but in spite of wicked men and the spirits of darkness, he boldly denounced the iniquities that prevailed.

The evil ones from the dark regions, which you term hell, had no power over Jesus my blessed master. Singly he withstood the black host. The chief priests, in order to excite the people against him, tried to fasten a charge on him as one who had his powers from Beelzebub—a being who had no existence but in their own ignorant imaginations. But they could not lay a finger on him. His work must first be done. Ah, why did these men shut their ears when he, the great teacher, spoke to them! And yet, there were always a few hearts open to receive the seed which he cast around. Some of the doctrines which he taught to the men of Judea had been preached in olden times, but they were new to them, and because they were new, these bigoted, conceited men would not listen to him—they were a priest-ridden race, content with that which they and their fathers had been taught.

One day we reached the outskirts of a village, when we met with one who was possessed, or what you would in your language, call mad. But he had a brain as sound as yours. It was not madness. We found him beset by a number of people, to whom he talked—sometimes as if an angel spoke, and then, directly, as a devil, making a jumble of the most holy and profane words; while the company who stood around him, tormented the poor man by hooting and laughter. As we looked on, pitying the condition of the victim, he cried out, 'Behold, there standeth amongst you three men who have just left the presence of the son of God! Hear ye them.' He had no sooner uttered these words than, possessed by another spirit, he broke out in a torrent of bitter curses against us. Feeling deeply for this distressed mortal, in the midst of his cursing, I commanded the spirits that possessed him, in the name of Jesus, to depart. The words were but spoken, when he who had just been raging like a wild beast, became like a lamb. The people stood amazed as they looked first at the man, and then at us. Then I spoke to them. I said we were but three men of flesh and blood like themselves; that there was nothing supernatural about us, being subject to the same experiences as they were; and though we had the power of doing that which they had just seen in the case of the man before them, they might also have the same power given to them. I then spoke to them concerning Jesus, and all that he was accomplishing in word and deed in Judea; and that it was from him, the prince of heaven and earth, who had been sent by the most high, we had the power to cast out devils. I talked to them of that God, that same God who had led their fathers of old, and who was now by His son, trying to lead them into the paths of truth and holiness. 'Look at this man,' I said, 'he now stands before you in his right mind, and will himself now speak to you.'

The poor man, first of all, lifted up his voice and thanked God, and then, turning to the people around him, told them that henceforth he would devote his life to the maintenance of the truths they had just heard uttered by those who had set him free. 'I now,' said he, 'know that I am a man. Hear, I pray you, what these men have yet to tell you; for I have been long lost to myself, and to all that has been going on in Judea and elsewhere.'

There was one thing, not understood by us at the time, that when any of these wonderful works were done by the disciples who were sent abroad on missions by the master for the preaching of the truth, he knew all that was taking place. It did not matter at what distance, our sayings and doings were known to him. It formed a subject of discussion amongst us how this could be—whether he had information through spirits in sympathy with him and us, or by some magnetic current or chain. Now, we know it was the latter. Not. only had he this gift, but when he saw fit, and conditions allowed, he could effect cures on diseased persons at a distance by the word of his mouth. And although we had the power of healing conferred on us from the most high, and exercised the gift, previous to our coming to Jesus, we in common with the rest of his followers, used his name when we put forth our powers.

This man, on whom the gracious power was exercised, had not only been educated in a high rank of life, but he was one who had been noble and good in character in the estimation of his neighbours. The consequence was, that during our stay at that place, which was for two or three days, a good work was begun. Some other marvellous works were done; and as our master had instructed us, we went into their synagogue, or place of meeting, and spoke to the assembled people.

The great and everlasting law of love was the chief subject of our addresses—a law not for one nation, but for all mankind; that this love was not only to be shown to our neighbours and friends, but to strangers, and even to our enemies. We impressed on them the necessity of holy living as the best preparation they could make for the great change that must come to all, when they could be called on to cast off the old clothing of the body, and be born again into the life of the spirit. We were glad to see that our labour was not in vain, for there were some in that place that professed to believe in the new views which we had set before them; and we went on our way, thanking God that we had been used by Him to bring back these souls from darkness to light.

Journeying towards Alexandria, we felt strengthened by the hope that in that city we would be enabled so to set forth our views, that a nucleus of organised effort would speedily be formed which would in a short time convert all Egypt to the faith of Jesus; that, by the sending out from the centre of teacher after teacher, the whole mass would be leavened with the doctrines of the master, and the Egyptian system completely overthrown. Men may build the finest and strongest of structures, but how often do we see them, by time and circumstances, levelled with the dust—heaps of ruins, telling to the beholder the sad tale. And so with us; the structure we were about to rear, and which was afterwards raised in Egypt, was by the time I left the body, almost overthrown, there being only a few here and there left to spread the good seed. Still, in spite of all hindrances, it must and shall be that the light which first broke out in Judea shall shine over Egypt and over all the earth.

Great opposition was experienced by us in our mission, but we never drooped. We knew that the work to be done must be accomplished step by step; the small stream would increase in breadth until it formed a sea, notwithstanding all opposition. Many of those who knew me joined themselves to us. Some of our converts were faithful: some of them fell back; while others, when persecution set in, became traitors, and were the first to turn and trample on us.

When in Alexandria we went to the temple of the Jews; but it was not to be compared in any way with the grand temple in Jerusalem. We read their sacred books, and pointed out in these the prophecies regarding the promised deliverer, how that all that had been said by the prophets of old concerning this coming one was fulfilled in him who had sent us to them, even Jesus, the son of Joseph the carpenter, who, by the power of the truths he taught, accompanied by his marvellous works, would deliver mankind from the slavery of sin and all its terrible consequences.

We had no thought of forming a church at that time. We allowed the Hebrew members of our little company (for we had formed a company) to go to the synagogues; but they were counselled to remember the truths taught by the master. We cared not whether they were Pharisees or Sadducees—one thing we required of them, to meet together daily for prayer, that the time might soon come when the true light should spread over all nations.

I had been nine months in Alexandria when it was determined by the brethren that I should return to Judea and give an account of the progress of our work. This I gladly undertook, for I was aware that the time was drawing near when our beloved master should leave us; for he had referred to it now and again when by ourselves, instructing us what we should do when he was taken from us. Sitting under the sycamore trees, I have listened to him while thus he spoke of going away; 'When I go to my kingdom, you will soon follow me. We shall not be long parted. But the work given me to do must first be done. My people may cast aside as worthless the truth I am sent to deliver unto them, but there are some who will open their ears; and that seed which I sow will yet spring up, and the harvest will be gathered on high in my kingdom in the heavens.'

I said I had been appointed by our company to return to Judea. We had amongst our number some rich men, farmers and others, and there was therefore no lack of means wherewith to send me back in a better outward condition than I had been in when I came to Egypt. I left wealthy, for I had a purple cloak and new sandals on my feet, with a well-filled purse in my girdle.

I embarked at Alexandria in a ship that was bound for Tyre. I might relate many of the incidents that occurred during the voyage across the great sea; but such tales, peculiar to all journeys, I must put aside—my great aim being to speak to you of Jesus and our mission. There was one incident however, that I must speak about.

We had been two or three days at sea, the sailors toiling hard at the sweeps, for the air was hot and close, when one of the ship's crew perceived a pirate vessel bearing down upon us. The ruthless robbers were nearing us, when our attention was drawn towards a dark column, no thicker than a man's waist, extending from the waters up into the heavens. We observed that just as the pirates were preparing to board us, the long, dark object we had seen gliding swiftly over the sea struck their ship, and down she went. We saw no more of her; but continued on our voyage in peace. I was not long left to wonder at what had taken place. My old and venerable friend, Issha, communicated with me in spirit, telling me that, seeing the coming danger, a number of spirits (who had, while in the body, belonged to a warlike tribe) interfered for our deliverance. They had formed a whirlwind which, rushing into a vacuum they had also produced, overwhelmed the robbers who were bent on our destruction. He told me how all this was done, but it was strange to me. He said; 'Be not afraid, my son; I am always ready to preserve thee from danger, and those who may be with thee in thy wanderings, not only on land, but on the waters also.'

At length we arrived at Tyre, where we landed. On joining once more the company of Jesus and his disciples, I was surprised and pleased, to find the man out of whom we had cast the devils had become a follower of the, master, and had been labouring with them in word and deed for about a year. On approaching Jesus, I was preparing to tell him all that had taken place since I left. But after welcoming me back, he showed me that he was well aware of what had taken place on my journeys, and also at Alexandria. 'Do not wonder,' he said, 'if I tell you that I know all that has happened to you. When I sent forth my brethren to declare the truth I have committed to them, I am not cut off from them, there is a communion kept up. There are also unseen ones at work, who are interested in that which you have got to do. When that work is done, even as mine is nearly finished, you will be welcomed to my kingdom; from thence you will be able to cast your eyes down to earth, where you will see men run on in sin, and feel that you are unable to do what you were wont to do while in the body. See, therefore, that you do all you can now, so that your joy may be great when you enter my kingdom and your kingdom.'

6

The crucifixion, resurrection and ascension of Jesus

The time was now fast approaching when Jesus would leave us; but, not as the shepherd leaves his flock, to become the prey of hungry wolves. No; though scattered over the wide world, we would not be exactly like deserted sheep; for the wolf-like persecutors of the brethren were, in truth, the very means by which the good seed was scattered abroad. The very winds of heaven carried the tidings of light and liberty to the peoples, who, groaning under the galling bondage of tyrants and priests, sprang up to renewed life: I would have said—never more to be enslaved. Doubtless the shackles would be struck off, but as in my vision, which I related to you, foreshowed, the time would come when even those freemen, lovers of light, having the truth, would get corrupted, become traffickers, making merchandise of God's truth—aye, selling it out in pennyworths to the starving, darkened souls of their fellow-men.

After my returning to the master, he visited various places in Judea, preaching and teaching in the synagogues: wherever he found an open door he took advantage of it. On these occasions he not only expounded the Hebrew writings concerning his coming, but directed the attention of his hearers to the prophecies and teachings in the writings of the nations around. But this was too much for the narrow-minded Jews, who would turn up their noses and walk out, leaving us the sole occupants of their meeting-house, and this because our master asserted that the men of other nations were, in the sight of God, equal with the Jews; that, notwithstanding their privileges as a nation, they were no better than their neighbours. How proud these men were of their forefathers, Abraham and Moses, and yet how unlike them in character! Well for them had they followed in the steps of those they professed to honour; but they were only too like the stiffnecked race which tormented the great prophet and lawgiver.

In travelling about Judea, we generally got shelter under the roof of some kind friend or other wherever we went. But there were times, and these were not seldom, when the sky was our only roof and the green sward our bed, while the moon smiled down on us as we slept under the jewelled canopy of the heavens above. At such times there were some of us who realised the presence of myriads of bright and lovely beings hovering around—aye, and ready to do battle on behalf of our lord and master. But he came not to force men into submission. (Had such been the case, I myself would have drawn the sword). He came to overcome enmity by love. I often thought at that time that his heart must have been sorely tried, when he observed some mean, sneaking fellows, who had been amongst the number he had so wonderfully fed, turning away from us when danger drew near, and when questioned, denying that they had ever got anything on such occasions. Ah! There are many such in the world yet, as I perceive,—men before whom heaven's clearest signs and wonder have been brought, but who, through the most contemptible cowardice, and fear of their fellow-men, shut their mouths and say nothing. However there were others, good men, who, though enduring a struggle, would in the end submit to be guided in the right course. I refer to certain educated men, occupying high places in the community, who, though somewhat faint-hearted, in their quiet hours sought for and received the truth. There were some of the same class who were continually hatching plans to entrap our beloved master in his words—something from which to form an accusation against him. Why? Because he spoke his mind: he declared, what they hated to hear—the truth, that if they turned not from their evil ways to follow in the steps of their fathers, Abraham, Isaac, and Jacob, who had listened to the voice of the lord, they would assuredly perish as a nation

The people of Judea, amid all their bitter sectarian strifes, looked for the speedy coming of their Messiah, but they could not see him in the lowly Nazarene. 'He! The son of a carpenter,' they cried. '*HE* the Messiah? No; our promised one will come as a king—our king. He will sweep earth of her kingdoms, and his dominion shall be from sea to sea.' They cast him off—this lowly, humble man; these vain and conceited men despised and rejected the chosen of God. Nursed on the bosom of a virgin, he was but a bastard in the eyes of the world. Yet he heeded not their scoffs and bitter hatred; for he knew that all the kingdoms of the world would submit to him; that those who had passed away, and generations yet to come, would all acknowledge him as their lord and king. Such, he maintained, was the meaning of the words spoken by the prophets of the olden time.

I have seen those crafty enemies of our beloved master often confounded by the wise sayings he uttered. On one occasion they thought to get him entangled in their web. They brought before him a poor woman taken in sin, and asked him to sit as judge in the case. The great Solomon was a wise man; but here was one of the wisest the world had ever seen, or would see; and what is his judgement? 'Let him who is sinless among you cast a stone at her!' O, had you but seen how these haughty priests and rulers looked when the Godlike sentence fell from the lips of Jesus. They had come into his presence, their eyes twinkling with malicious intent, sure of thrusting him into a corner; but when they heard the words of the master they slunk off, one after another, sheepish and confounded. That was a lesson for them, and for all. Examine yourselves and see if you can afford to cast dirt at your neighbour? That is how the master administered justice. O that he were followed by the judges of the earth! He who sitteth as a judge should, before he condemns, look into himself, to see if in any way he is upholding the system that has brought the criminal to the bar of judgment. Such were the kind of lessons imparted to us by our master, and which we treasured up for the future.

In all our wanderings, he never lost an opportunity of doing good. But even in this his enemies sought to find fault in him. 'Why should your master heal on a sabbath-day?' So blinded were these men by their hair-splitting subtleties regarding forms and ceremonies, that they saw not the absurdity involved in their question. They saw not that nothing should be allowed to interfere with the doing of that which was good in itself and beneficial to man. The rest-day was undoubtedly a wise law, good for man, and a blessing even to the beast of burden. It was for man's welfare that the great and good father appointed it; and yet these blinded enemies of Jesus found fault with him because he had healed an afflicted mortal on the sabbath-day! The creator makes no difference in days; every day is a day for serving Him—every day a day for doing good. The sabbath is a gracious arrangement, affording man a resting-time, in which his thoughts may be drawn upwards, from the temporal to the spiritual—a time for clearing away the rubbish of the six days, and acquiring bodily and mental strength. But such a day was never intended to be wholly devoted to fasting and prayer. That would be a breach of the law of rest. True worship is not confined to set times; and God demands from man no more than he is able to give: to serve Him with all the powers of which he is possessed. Thus Jesus, my master, taught us, and had his lessons been heeded, the world would have been this day nearer to God.

The light is beginning to break all over the spirit world. That one of whom Hafed has spoken will shortly arise: a poor man in the eyes of the worldling, but endowed with great and wondrous power who will overthrow all those sys- tems,—political, social, and religious, that stand in the way of truth. I can perceive through the medium I am at present making communication through, that you live in an age (then 1875) of advanced education, and that brilliant stars are shining and giving light to the world. But this coming one, of whom I now speak, will not appear in that way. He will not come from the schools of the learned. He will speak under spirit power. The voice that will be heard, will be that of a mighty angel: then will be heard the crash of false systems, all over the earth, under his mighty wheels; and then all will worship the one great father, though under a different name. But I must hasten on.

As I have said, there were some amongst the rulers and chief priests, who scrupled not to use the vilest means to find an accusation against our blameless master. But in their assembly, one of their number, named Nicodemus, stood boldly up in his defence, and showed that Jesus was really what he professed to be—the sent of God. But the saying of the master about the destruction and restoration of the temple—meaning his body—was caught up by them, and denounced as a crime by the priests. What! Talk about the destruction of their great and gorgeous temple, the glory of their world! This was not passed over. These priests, in their robes of more than regal magnificence, resolved to crush this outcast in appearance, but the true high priest. These men were not stupid; they knew what they were about. If the doctrines of Jesus prevailed, they knew well their trade was at an end. No longer would they feast their eyes on the poverty-stricken people dragging up sheep to hand over to them to be slain as a sacrifice, and then eaten by them! Ah, well I know how those things were done. The priests were all alike in all nations.

I have no intention to notice all that was said and done in relation to our beloved master, seeing that you already have a good deal of information from those who were in closer contact than I was. But what I do give freely to you, see that you give as freely to others. O many and precious were the sayings he uttered before he left us, and in all he said, we saw that he was deeply impressed with that which was coming upon him. But he was ever anxious to impress on us that though removed from our sight, he would still watch over us till we entered the kingdom above. Were the whole kingdoms of the world to become subject to him (as yet they shall be) what are all these compared with his kingdom of the spirit world! O that the nations of earth would but submit to his easy yoke! All that he asks often is, that they should aspire to higher life get nearer and ever nearer to God their father.

We were in Galilee when the passover of the Jews drew nigh; and we were surprised when the master said to us that he would go up to Jerusalem on the occasion. We tried to persuade him against going; for we knew that the chief priests and others had been plotting to destroy him. They saw clearly that if Jesus succeeded in getting the people to submit to his doctrines, their whole system would be overthrown, and that their fat livings, upheld by exactions from the ignorant masses, would also be swept away. But, to all our entreaties, the master would not lend his ear. He had made up his mind to do his duty, and go he would. Ah, there was no shrinking, no cowardly fear in him when danger was impending. It mattered not where he was—whether in the temple or synagogue, on hillside or seaside, he never showed the slightest fear of man, but was ever ready to speak and work for man's welfare. Finding him resolved we opposed him no longer, but catching the same spirit, we professed, one and all of us, to be ready to go even to death with him. So we thought then. O how brave we are at times! But it was self that made us cowards.

When we reached Jerusalem, he went to the temple, as was his wont, and spoke daily to the people there assembled, at that time in great numbers. In the evenings he went to Kedron, in the gardens of which we found shelter, though under the open canopy of heaven, away from the noise and bustle of the city. The crisis came on. The last evening with our master, after supping with him, we went back to our shelter in the gardens. And while engaged in devotion with him there, the chief priests and rulers were sitting in council, as we afterwards learned, planning how they might get rid of him. But even amongst these men there were some who had secretly believed in Jesus; and now that the storm was about to burst, they boldly avowed their attachment, and stood up in his defence. These were, Nicodemus, Joseph of Arimathea, Gamaliel, and others of the masters of Israel. The high priest Caiaphas, as I afterwards learned, rose from his great throne and spoke to the assembled council. After showing what Jesus had done and was doing, he accused him of witchcraft, stating that witnesses were ready to declare that he had spoken both against their holy temple and city, and that he had despised the laws of Moses—laws that had been penned by the hand of God. Another rose and accused him of making himself a king, thus giving the Roman government cause for complaint and interference; while one after another brought other charges against him, and clamorously called for instant decision.

It was at this point the humble and meek-minded Gamaliel opened his mouth in defence of the master. He asked them how it was possible for such a character as they made Jesus out to be, to do the good and wonderful works he had done, and of which many of them were witnesses, except God were with him? Thereupon one rose up in great wrath, as if possessed by their supreme devil Beelzebub, and appealed to heaven to crush the meek Gamaliel. But the ruler Nicodemus boldly stood up, and quietly but firmly thrust back accusations that had been made against Jesus. He said he would not call down the curses of heaven on their heads he would rather plead for mercy on them, notwithstanding the iniquitous courses they had pursued to gain their object—the destruction of the innocent. 'O blessed religion, as taught by Jesus, glittering in the beauty of truth,' he cried. 'But when put on as a cloak, it becomes dark and cruel seeking to appease offended heaven by sacrifices on the bloody altars. This is not the religion taught by Jesus. Why do you thus secretly meet to sit in judgment on him? He is not afraid to look you in the face. Are ye afraid? But go on in your evil way, and become guilty of slaying the innocent. Rear your altar, ye priests! Lead forth as the victim, for the last of your bloody sacrifices, Jesus, the son of the living God!' Thus spake the ruler, who had long been a believer in secret, but who now fought bravely for the master before the chief priests and rulers of the nation. 'I leave you,' he said; 'I wash my hands of this evil deed!' On saying which, accompanied by Joseph, Gamaliel, and others, he left the council. That same Caiaphas would have given a hundred years of life could he have done the same; but he was afraid for his position as high priest.

Not far from the place of secret council was Judas, the wretched traitor, who sold his master for a few pieces of silver. My soul burned with bitter wrath against the foul wretch, and had he been clinging even to the sacred altar, I verily believe I would have torn him limb from limb, and thought I was but doing justly. The traitor lay waiting the decision of the secret conclave, some of whom had concerted with him that same night how to take Jesus.

A sorrowful night it was to us all. He alone was composed. He was conversing freely with us of the heavenly country, and of his return to his kingdom above, when lo! In the thick darkness, we saw lights approaching. All nature was silent, even the stars veiled their faces, refusing to look on the impending deed of darkness. O think of that! The lights of flickering flambeaus showed the forms that approached, guided by the traitor: a band armed with swords and spears and bows—a whole regiment of armed men to capture one man and a few unarmed followers. Jesus stood unmoved at the sight, and when they came near, he said, 'Whom seek ye?'

They said they wanted Jesus of Nazareth. He then said, 'I am he,' when at once, as if stricken, the whole band of armed men fell flat on their faces to the ground. Amazing sight! The rough soldiers of Rome, unaccustomed to bowing the knee, doing homage as to a king—prostrate before him whom they had come to arrest as a criminal! Then the traitor, who accompanies them to earn his vile wages, attempts to salute his master whom he had sold (a long and sore punishment he had to undergo, and he had doubtless long regretted the dreadful deed). At length, they laid hands on the victim, when Peter, who was armed with a sword, boldly attacked them, wounding severely a servant of the high priest. But even then, at that trying moment, the goodness and power of our beloved master was shown; for, after rebuking the impulsive but warm-hearted disciple, he turned to the man who had been struck, and by a touch healed his wound. Ah. Caiaphas, where was the sorcery there? The after-life of the man whose wound had been healed, gave answer; for he became from that night a thorough believer in Jesus, and was prominent as a spreader of the truth in Judea. That passionate stroke of Peter's made numerous converts to the truth—more than ever he had made during all the mission of the master.

They led him away, and brought him before the high priest and rulers, who ordered him to be taken to Herod's judgment-bar; but he, declining to sit in judgment on Jesus, handed him over to Pilate the Roman governor. Being a foreigner, I was not suspected of being one of his followers, and got admission along with others. There the enemies of Jesus brought forward their charges, one of these being that he had said he was a king, thinking by such an accusation to gain the ear of the Roman governor. But after questioning him, Pilate declared to the clamorous, malicious men who crowded the Roman hall, that he could find nothing against him. You can imagine how hard it was for me to stand there, amidst the crowd of bitter enemies, and see my beloved master rudely struck in the face, while first one miscreant and then another brought forward false accusations against him.

Pilate, who was a just and honourable man, fearing the gods of his country, indignantly protested against the bigotry of these spiteful Jews, and declared that he saw nothing in their charges. But they, determined to accomplish their object, insinuated that he was not doing his duty as a Roman governor in setting one at liberty who had been seditiously stirring up the people. Still he stood firm, even condescending to plead with them to desist from their charges. 'Away with the fellow! Crucify him!' cried the infuriated crew. Even the wife of Pilate entreated him not to listen to the bloodthirsty accusers of Jesus; but though he considered him innocent, he—afraid of the threats of the Jewish rulers and priests to denounce him to the imperial government—after protesting against the deed, and washing his hands from innocent blood, gave him up to be crucified. He was guilty, notwithstanding: for, but for his cowardly fear of Jewish malevolence, he had power sufficient to have acquitted Jesus. But in all, this was fulfilled the old prophecy that he would die an ignominious death.

There was no prison for him—no breathing-time allowed by these hounds thirsting for his blood. The altar was erected and the victim lamb was led out as a bloody sacrifice to the God of heaven! Ah, what have not priests done in the name of God to further their own selfish ends! Alas! It has ever been thus: True religion set at nought; love and truth sacrificed!

That morning you would have thought that all Judea had gathered together to witness the crucifixion of these three men; for Jesus was doomed to suffer death between two robbers: thus basely heaping odium on him even in his death. I never left from the time of the arrest till they brought him to Calvary. I had seen nothing of the others, excepting Peter, who was present at the palace of the high priest in the early morning. Poor Peter, he lost his temper when questioned by one who suspected him to be a follower of Jesus, denying with an oath all knowledge of him; but bitterly he repented of his cowardly conduct.

Jerusalem was, at that time, crowded by people from all parts of Judea, and the whole course of the ever-memorable procession along the streets was crowded by onlookers; and when the Roman guards on their prancing horses appeared with Jesus in their midst, many of the people wept; and some of those who had cried for his crucifixion now shed tears as they looked on him who quietly and uncomplainingly went on to a cruel and shameful death.

On reaching the accursed hill they stripped him of his rainment, and drove the nails through his hands and feet into the cross; and doing the same with the two robbers, they thrust the three crosses into the ground. And there between these two thieves hung the prince of glory in agony and shame amid that crowd of mocking heartless Jews and rough Roman soldiers, yet even then I heard no complaint from his lips. On the cross over his head, the Romans, by command of Pilate, placed an inscription, in three languages, evidently to spite the Jews, in these words: 'Jesus of Nazareth the king of the Jews.' They complained to Pilate, and wished him to alter it, but he refused to hear them.

The sun had shone out beautifully over the magnificent city on the morning of that terrible day. Could it be possible that a deed so atrocious could have been perpetrated? Yet he still continued to pour down his beams on the crowds that stood around the hill of Calvary—where the sent of God hung up as a spectacle for the world to gaze at. But the cruel process of crucifixion had not long been enacted when the heavens were overcast, and all nature became black as if a pall had been flung over the whole sky. The sun ashamed, hid his face in thick clouds. The forked lightnings darted athwart the dark expanse, and the thunder rolled fearfully, north, south, east, and west. We felt the earth quaking beneath our feet. The Roman guards stood motionless, gazing in silence on the fearful scene, while the crowds of Jews slunk away in consternation towards the city. So furious was the storm that terror was seen on many a face, and an educated Roman was heard to say, 'Surely this man is the son of a divine being.'

Amongst those who continued to stand by, I observed a number of the followers of our beloved master; and we drew together, keeping close to the cross, on which he hung in agony. While he lived, he continued to look down on us, while now and again we heard words of comfort coming from his lips. Although some even of the twelve had timidly deserted him, not one of the women who had so devotedly followed him was absent; and some of those who stood firm to the close were strangers like myself. Ah! these were trying, painful hours to us who looked on. To see one who we esteemed as the chosen of God for the world's good, crucified in pain and shame, and set up between two criminals! But even these two dying men, amid their own grievous agonies, praised him who hung between. They had witnessed his childlike submission, they had heard his words of love and deep compassion—his prayer for his murderers; and being near to death, their eyes were opened to discern the thousands of the spirit world hovering around. That mailed host spoken of by Hafed was there too, who, had our dying Lord but whispered to them, could have swept Jerusalem and its inhabitants into utter destruction. But no; such was not his way of overcoming enmity. He prayed to the great father to forgive them. Some of those men stood looking at him whom they had treated thus, imagined that he would miraculously free himself from the cross and had he done so, they would have bent the knee to him and acknowledged him as the Messiah; but he would not; the work had to be done, and that was to sacrifice himself—to die for the truth he had been sent to proclaim.

During the great darkness, it was said that the spirits of men who had long passed away, appeared to many in Jerusalem. There were some so silly as to say that they had resumed their old bodies that had lain for ages in the grave. If they appeared at all, it must have been in the bodies materialised for the occasion.

As night drew on, we left the place of crucifixion; but others of our company, with the women, still knelt round the cross. They were thus kneeling when the soldiers approached to break the limbs of the crucified, before the Jewish sabbath began. Finding that Jesus was dead, they did nothing. The blessed spirit was away to paradise, whence he would return to impart comfort and instruction to his sorrowing followers. The two malefactors, who still lived, were quickly put out of their dreadful agonies by the soldiers. These men, as I afterwards learned, entered into the third sphere, and are now blessed evangelists, labouring amongst the denizens of the dark caverns. He too had gone there, and traversed the dreary mazes of the great prison-house, because he desired to pass through all the experiences of man, so that he might the better accomplish the work of redemption. And yet though coming through such experiences, he ever remained pure and unblameable. In whatever place he was—Greece, Egypt, Persia, or elsewhere—it was the same: he conformed to the laws of people, but worshipped God, the great spirit.

A number of us met on the evening of that sad day in the house of one of the brethren. You can imagine the heavy hearts we had. But it was a night of prayer; and as the sabbath came on we felt as if Jesus himself were there in spirit. When it was told to us in the morning that Joseph of Arimathea, who had so boldly defended him in the council, had got possession of the body of our master, we rejoiced greatly. But this did not banish the thought that he who had loved us was now taken away from our mortal sight. It was while we were in this condition, that the venerable form of Issha appeared to me, and told me not to be disquieted, that Jesus would soon be with us again, and that the angelic host would watch over us till he returned to give us the power which he had promised.

All Jerusalem was now in commotion because of that which had taken place the day before. The priests, pondering on the few words that had fallen from the lips of Jesus regarding his rising again, got a guard of soldiers to watch the tomb where Joseph had laid the body, lest, as they said, we should steal it away, and say he had risen again. Poor men! They knew not (but they might have known from their sacred writings) that all the legions of Rome could not keep him entombed—aye, though he had been built up in a solid pyramid, that would not have prevented the son of the highest coming back to his sorrowing brethren.

And when the sabbath was past, and the morning light came on, does the great deliverer burst out upon these soldiers in the greatness of his power? No; he quietly passes through the doorway, and in the sight of the trembling guards, who bow before him, he leaves them to watch an empty tomb. The soldiers, on recovering from their astonishment that which they had seen, went and reported to the priests all that had taken place. And what did these evil-hearted men? It was said that they attempted to bribe the poor soldiers to say that, while they slept, the body of Jesus was taken away by his disciples—'Only do this, and we will make it allright with your commander,' for well they knew that it was death by the Roman law for a soldier to sleep while on guard.

Such were the men who crucified our master. Chief priests in the temple of God! Dastards to tempt poor soldiers with a bribe. Ah, why should they thus try to hide the truth? It would not hide. They had but to look at the rent veil of their temple to see heaven's own condemnation of their deed. Did such a thing ever happen before Who did it? Will they blame us for that too! It was no earthly power that did that. The fire of heaven cleft it in twain, a word went forth—away with all these mummeries! The day of symbols is past. Not now by these may man approach his maker. Man's heart is the true temple of God. Conscience will guide man the lesser intelligence to serve God the great intelligence. And Jesus the light of the world will, in spirit, destroy the corrupt systems of men.

All that sabbath-day we were continually coming and going—we could not rest. The room in which we met was never without some of us on our knees in prayer. At last, on the morning after, we were astonished when it was reported to us that some of the brethren had seen the master; and thereafter, when we met with some others in the house where I lodged, my venerable father Issha appeared before us, and as distinctly visible as one of ourselves. He put forth his hands as we sat, and at once before our wondering eyes stood Jesus in bodily form. He stretched out his hands, and thereon we saw the wounds the nails had made. And then he spoke to us, 'I have been away and have seen my kingdom, and now I will be with you for a short time before I finally depart.'

There were some who thought it was a vision. But I knew it was a reality. I saw that it was the same body on which I had so often looked before the crucifixion; and yet there was some difference, not easily described. But when grasped by the hand, the feeling was the same as when we grasped the hands of each other. He appeared to be sadder now than formerly: though he rarely ever smiled. (When a boy, he was joyous and laughed like the rest of us). But now, he spoke with solemnity. He alluded to the opposition that would be made to our work, but told us not to be afraid, for he would be with us; that when persecution set in against us because of the truth, we were to watch lest we should be tempted to fall away. 'Be ever bold and faithful in the work which I have given you to do; never withhold your hands from the great work. A structure will be raised; but a time will come when my doctrine will be trampled under foot by men professing to be my true followers, but hypocritical worshippers, wearing a cloak of truth to cover their iniquity.'

Again and again he met with us, and spoke of the necessity of prayer and watchfulness on our part, in view of the mission we were undertaking. These interviews with our beloved master were held in various places, when we came together, during three or four weeks; but none of us knew where he went to when he left us. He had been seen by some of the brethren, who were fishermen, walking on the sea; by others, on Mount Olive; while I and others had seen him surrounded by heavenly hosts. Indeed, it may be said that he met with the brethren by day, and with the angels by night. I had seen these holy ones in their mortal form; but with Jesus they appeared in spirit with a brightness beyond that of the sun at noonday.

As the day drew nigh when he should leave us, he gave each of us directions about the work we had undertaken. Although the Jews had cut him off, we were not (he said) to cast that in their teeth, and refuse to deal with them; on the contrary, we were to hold forth his truths to the people of Jerusalem. If they should revile us because of our faith in him, we were to submit, answering them not. And there were some of us who needed this advice of the master. I know I had a fiery temper; but, bearing his words in mind, I succeeded in curbing it, even though, in doing so, I had to bite my lip. Better to do that than give the enemy anything to say. Indeed, to become a successful preacher of the master's truth, this course had to be carried out.

We went out that day with him into the country, but even then, as we journeyed onwards, the country people drew near to us, and he put forth his power, as he had done before, and healed those who were sick among them. At length we came to the spot whence he was to be taken from us. We stood around him, while he prayed for us; and just as he was in the act of blessing us, he was gradually lifted up before our eyes. Gazing longingly upwards, we beheld a host of bright beings overshadowing us, amongst whom I saw my beloved father Issha.

As the form of our lord and master rose, it seemed slowly to dissolve, and a cloud came down and shut out our view. We saw no more of Jesus, our beloved master; but we knew we would meet him in the heavens, into which he had gone, and that, though no longer with us in the body, he would be with us in spirit to direct and guide us. It was a foretaste of heaven. We went back to Jerusalem, as he had bidden us, to wait in his promise—the fullness of spirit.

7

The work goes on. Persecution begins

The rulers of the Jews thought they had for ever destroyed our cause, laid it in the dust, by taking away our master — that they would hear no more about it because he was dead. Dead! poor blinded men, they were not aware that the truth could never die. But we kept quiet, waiting for the fulfilment of his promise. There were some, however, of our number that did not even then comprehend his meaning. They thought that he would yet appear as the saviour of the nation from bondage. But there were others of us who knew better. We knew that his appearance would be spiritual; that he referred to the gift of the spirit which he would bestow on us, so that we might be fully prepared to go out to the world and proclaim the truths which he had taught us. I, who was in possession of some of the gifts with which all were afterwards endowed, and others who were not so privileged, but who understood the words of the master, endeavoured to keep up the hearts of the brethren in our daily meetings for prayer. Not an hour passed over us that saw not some of us in prayer. We ceased not in our supplications to the most high, that He would send forth His holy ones to guard us from our enemies, who, like lions, lay ready to spring on us.

At length the day came on — a day I can never forget. We were all assembled in the usual place, engaged in solemn prayer, when the walls of the house were terribly shaken, as if by an earthquake, while lights of a blueish-white colour blazed above our heads; but beyond these strange lights we saw the prince, our master, in glory, surrounded by bright hosts of spirits. And while we gazed in wonder and amazement, the bright lights that had been flickering above us fell on our heads, and then it was we felt the promise was fulfilled — that we had received power from the highest to fit us for our work. Thus were we equipped by our beloved master, ready to do battle for him with the sword of the spirit.

It was one of the Hebrew festivals, when thousands were gathered together in Jerusalem from all the surrounding nations, and we went out and proclaimed the truth about Jesus to crowds of the people in all the different languages. The effect on the minds of many was deep and lasting, and productive of much good; for these strangers were from other lands, in returning to their homes, they carried the truth with them, and thus became the pioneers of those of us who were to follow. And it was not long before they were followed; for, from that day when so many were drawn to listen to us, persecution set in. Some of our number were imprisoned; but their prison doors were flung open by unseen hands. The Jewish rulers were confounded; they knew not what to do, so as to keep the common people in ignorance of such wonderful works. They seemed afraid that the populace would rise in rebellion against the Roman government, and thus bring down the heavy hand of Rome on the heads of the nation. But the result was that many of the brethren were compelled to fly from Jerusalem.

The chosen disciples and others who remained proposed to form a council for the management of the work. I felt myself bound to oppose this, and entreated them not to interfere with the liberty of each other, that we should go out, two or three together, as the spirit directed us, uncontrolled by the rules of a council, who might in time seek to exercise lordship over brethren who were called to labour in distant countries. There should be but one master, I maintained, and each and all guided by his spirit what to do and how to do is. But my counsel was rejected: some would not listen to me. I saw the greater number was against me, and I agreed to submit. I said however, that if I saw the spirit of lordship getting up, I would have nothing more to do with them, but go out to the world and work freely in the cause of Jesus, my only master. Certain rules for the ongoing of the work in Jerusalem were adopted.

In Jerusalem they had all things in common—that is, rich and poor fared alike—all were on the level of brotherhood, and all were glad to do the master's work.

The council was composed principally of the Hebrew disciples, with a few like myself from other countries. Here were some dark-skinned sons of Africa; there a sleek-haired native of India; and there were some even from your own islands of the far west. In such a mixed assembly it would have been strange had nothing occurred to disturb us. The Hebrews being in the greatest numbers, would have their own way, the impetuous Peter contending strongly for the observance by the brethren of certain Jewish rites and ceremonies. Violent discussions, in which some hot words were uttered, almost led to blows; for a number of us who were strangers, who had drank in the master's doctrines of freedom, were determined to crush this attempt of the Jewish brethren to bring us under the yoke of Judaism. We maintained that such national distinctions should be thrust aside, as opposed to the doctrines proclaimed by Jesus himself, which were not for the Jews only, but for the whole world. But the council, as constituted, had not a lengthened existence; for in the heat of the persecution, it was broken up, and all were compelled to wander into various countries.

I went to Greece. I was alone, and I felt myself free to act as the spirit directed me. It was a common thing in Greece at that time for men of learning to frequent places of public resort, and discuss various subjects of interest in morals and philosophy. To such places I went and, as opportunity offered, took part in the discussions, but having always before me the main object of my life—the truth concerning Jesus. I knew my duty, and was fixed in my determination that it should never be neglected. I was a stranger, an outcast Egyptian, with no one to care for me; but I felt myself more at liberty than ever I was to advocate the doctrines of my master; aye, and ready to die for them; for well I knew of the happy home he had in keeping for me in his kingdom above.

I first visited Athens, and after sojourning there for a time, I resolved to go to Rome, being anxious to see the magnificent city; but I did not see it after all, for on my way I was led by the spirit to land in Sicily; from there I went to Smyrna, and back again to Athens.

I spoke in general in public assemblages. Amongst the subjects of discussion at these gatherings of the philosophers of Greece, that of the Hebrew Jesus and his doctrines was frequently introduced. So far as outward appearance went, there was little to recommend me to the notice of these philosophers. My clothing was such that some of them treated. me as a beggar, and without being solicited would give me a small piece of money. I had been proud, but I was not then. I knew now the value of the smallest coin; for if I required it not for myself, there were many a poor helpless one to be found on the wayside who would be glad of the gift. It was well with me, in such cases, that I had the spiritual power of mind-reading, for there were then, as I suppose there are now, sham beggars, who imposed on their fellowmen. I quietly sat and heard these philosophers discussing about my master Jesus and his doctrines, waiting patiently to hear them give their verdict thereon. I would then step forward (they knew me only as an Egyptian) and say, 'Sirs, I have seen this Hebrew about whom you have been speaking,' and then they would invite me to speak concerning him. Thus encouraged, I entered at once into the history of Jesus, for of this I could speak freely, and then related to them all that I had seen him do, of the wonderful powers he put forth on behalf of man; and also or the wisdom that was displayed in the words which fell from his mouth; of his blameless life, his cruel and shameful death at the hands of his own countrymen, his appearance to his disciples, and his glorious ascension. I contended that in Jesus we found the great deliverer long promised to the nations—one who, in his character and teachings, was greater than Socrates and other famous teachers who had passed away. I generally received an attentive hearing on these occasions, while some of my hearers would kindly take me to his own home, where I was invited to use the baths, provided with suitable clothing, and made welcome as a guest. I felt thankful for such treatment, and hesitated not on such occasions to accept the hospitality offered. But though sadly in need of clothing, I could not lay aside my old cloak, the same that I had worn when with Jesus. I was determined to keep it till it became my shroud, for I more than suspected that there was a virtue in that old and well-worn garment. I had used it as a coverlet on the bed of the sick, and when the patient waked up from the calm sleep which my old cloak had produced, the fever was gone. So I never lost sight of my cloak. Thanks to my master, I was also in possession of the gifts of spiritual sight and hearing, of healing, and of prophecy, all which I exercised whenever I saw an opportunity of doing good to my fellow-men.

In the midst of all my labours in Greece and other parts, thoughts of hope would spring up. But the difficulties that beset me, and the persecution that followed hard at my heels, drove me sometimes into a state of despondency, in which I lost hope of seeing Egypt again, and at times, for a minute of two, I thought my brain was deranged, or that it was all a dream; but it was but momentary, for I would hear a voice which at once freed me from my gloomy thoughts. The whispers of the angel, thank God, opened my eyes, and I saw that there could be no derangement, and that I was as much a man as I ever was.

8

Rejection in Egypt. Reunited with Issha in spirit

The proclamation of the new faith in many places had been attended with varied degrees of success. In some cases cruel persecution had followed in its track. Some of us had been stoned and shamefully treated—hunted like wild beasts from place to place. For a while after our arrival in a city, no molestation would be offered by any one; but, as impressions began to be made on the minds of the citizens in favour of the new life and liberty of thought in regard to things spiritual, the priests would get alarmed. They saw that, if our doctrines got lodged in the hearts of the people, then their wretched systems would be uprooted, their coffers emptied, and they and their disgusting mummeries swept away. In this they were but doing the work of priestcraft at all times; for, whenever and wherever the truth interfered with their power over the minds of the people, these priests crushed it beneath their heel. It matters not in what nation, or in what age of the world, rather than lose the upper hand, the priests have brought the people down to a level with the beasts—buried them up in ignorance and silly superstitions. How often have I tried to shut out that which I had seen in vision, that a time would come when even the professed followers of Jesus—priests of the *Christian* faith—would do the very same thing! I strove to keep out that black future, but it would not. O cruel mockery of Jesus and his truth!

I resolved at last to leave Greece, where I had been labouring for a long time, and return to Egypt. Many years of trial and trouble had passed over me since I left the ancient temple in Thebes, where I had spent many happy hours with my beloved and venerable father Issha, who, though absent in the body, was often with me in spirit. At length, after a season of alternate triumph and defeat in my labours on my homeward journey, I arrived on the banks of the Nile. On entering Thebes, I noticed that the destroyer had been at work. Many of the inhabitants had been driven off, and houses were falling into ruins. I directed my steps to the temple, but no one seemed to know me. When I told them who I was, I was repulsed, scorned, and treated as an apostate. I had no desire to become a wanderer again; so, in spite of their opposition, I resolved to remain, for I began to feel age creeping on me, although not what you would call an old man. My hair was getting grey—the snow was whitening the mountain-top.

I was more successful with the common people, some of whom had known or heard of the venerable Issha; and when I told them the story of Jesus—his connection with Egypt and Issha, his life and death in Judea, and the sufferings we had endured on behalf of the truth they began to give ear to me, and to drink in the truths I proclaimed. For a while I continued to exhort them, setting before. them lessons fitted to lead them in the ways of goodness and truth. In course of time a few came together and bound themselves as a church, and I spent some happy days with them as their shepherd. It was not till two of my old fellow priests, who had been companions of my youth, joined our small community, that opposition began to show itself; but through the kind offices of the church in Alexandria, which at that time was large and influential, we received favour. It was in Thebes that I first baptised converts from the Egyptian faith, and observed the lord's supper.

It was at this time that I was visited by the venerable Hafed, who recounted to me many interesting experiences in connection with the master and his work. It was a glorious time for me to sit in the company of such a man: for, excepting Jesus our master, I never, in all my travels, met with one so full of the spirit as Hafed prince of Persia. His stay was but short; for he knew, he said, the work that was still before him, and the sufferings to be endured, before he finished his course. At his departure, we gave what we could to him and the two companions in attendance on him. It was not much, for we were poor in the world's goods. Eighteen or twenty of us went on with them the first day's journey; and at sunset we assembled for prayer. That was a glorious night for us: indeed, it was like a heaven on earth. We were all in the spirit—no longer hedged in by the barriers of earth, but in paradise itself. Instead of eighteen or twenty, we found ourselves in the company of tens of thousands of happy ones; while our ears were ravished by the music of the heavenly choirs. Words fail me to describe the wonderful vision of that night.

Though a Christian and follower of Jesus (for that name was beginning to be applied to us), Hafed, at the rising of the next morning, as he had been taught, bent himself in prayer before the symbol of him who is the source of all light and life. After prayer, we bade him and his two companions farewell; and his parting words were. 'Farewell! We will meet again in the land beyond!' They went on their way and we went back to Thebes. We had been greatly cheered and strengthened, and we resolved to give ourselves continually to prayer, so that we might obtain aid from on high, and be more fitted for the good work; for I knew well that the time was approaching when help would be needed. I knew that we would not be wholly driven out: there would always be some left. As the seed scattered on the waters brought forth abundantly in due season, so would the truth which we had preached spring forth in good to men and glory to our great master.

We were getting strong in numbers, the new doctrines spreading over the community; and the name 'Christians' was taken by us in good part; for truly it was a grand name. The members of the church were of acknowledged good character; chaste always; no one could point the finger at them; and they were ever ready to help the needy and clothe the naked. And so we began to be looked up to. But just then the priests got alarmed at the position we had attained. If this continued, they would at last be swamped; for their money was falling away. The people showed their indifference towards the old system, and could no longer be hoodwinked by the silly mummeries and gaudy processions of the priests. So they brought all their power to bear against us. I had been comfortable, and beginning to think all well, forgetting all that had been foreshown me in my vision. Had I pondered on that, I would have seen the folly of cherishing the idea of enjoying a quiet and comfortable life.

The priests, though bitterly opposed to us, were wary, they did not dare to lift a finger against any of the brethren, for they had secured favour of the people generally; but they determined to get rid of me. I was seized and cast into a dungeon, and thereafter taken from it, led out of the city, and forbidden to enter it. I was a banished man! Once more a wanderer. The little flock, thus deprived of its shepherd, was scattered. Strong-minded as I had ever been, this reverse was too much for me—I sat down by the wayside and wept. I thought my heart would burst. I felt I was a dying man. In my soreness of heart, I even cried to the prince to come to my help and crush those men who had risen up against me. Alas! In the bitterness of my spirit I forgot that the sword of truth was the only one that can be wielded. A few of the brethren followed after me, and we journeyed through the mountainous districts of the Red Sea into Arabia. After wandering hither and thither, preaching and teaching wherever we got the opportunity, we turned our faces towards Egypt—our home.

We were still wandering homewards, when one day I felt that my voice, that had all along been so powerful, had become weak. I was no longer able to engage in that which I had so long taken pleasure in. The end, I felt, was fast approaching; and one morning I told my companions that before the setting of the sun I would leave them. With sorrowful faces they gathered around me, and recovering my voice, I spoke to them with all my wonted energy. I counselled them to go back to Thebes, and endeavour to draw the scattered people together, telling my two old companions (the priests) to look well to the flock, and promised that though absent from them in body, I would be present with them in spirit. After embracing them one by one, I lay down with my old cloak wrapped round me. I fell asleep. When I opened my eyes, before me stood my beloved old father, Issha.

At first, I could not conceive what had happened. Was it a dream—a vision? But gradually I began to realise my change. I was at length in the paradise of the blessed. I looked around, and I saw on a hill a grand and beautiful building. I questioned my venerable friend in regard to all that I cast my eyes on, and could hardly take time to get his answers, so eager was I to obtain information. At length he brought me before the prince, Jesus my beloved master. I dared not lift my eyes to look on him then, but bent myself in deepest reverence—for I was dazzled by the exceeding glory that surrounded him. But joyfully and with outstretched arms he embraced me, and welcomed me to that glorious kingdom he had so often spoken of while he was with me in the body.

Thus my friends, I have accomplished that which I promised. May the Almighty direct you in all your ways, so that you may receive the welcome of the great prince into his kingdom above!

Questions Answered

by

HAFED

Q. Can you tell us anything about the book of Job, as given in the Hebrew scriptures?

A. I have seen the story of Job in the books of the Chaldeans. It is possible that Moses saw it in these, and being an acute and learned man, he would very quickly see the benefit that might be derived from its publication amongst his people.

Q. What was the doctrine taught by the magi in regard to the world?

A. In their sacred books the Persians taught that spirits existed before all worlds; that there were three kinds of spirit—the immortal, the genii, and the mortal; that the son was the first of the immortal spirits, and was placed over the spirit world of our planetary system before taking human form; that as mankind had fallen from their allegiance to him, it became him, who was their great lord, to take on himself a mortal body, and endeavour by his example and precept to draw them back to himself.

Q. Were you impressed by the size and grandeur of the Egyptian temples?

A. They were almost all in a ruinous state when I visited Egypt. It was not time however that had laid them low, so much as war. When invaded by foreign armies the people flocked to the temples, thinking to get shelter there and help from the gods, and they generally carried their wealth with them. When their enemies became aware of this, they were all the more determined to subdue them; and thus these famous structures became arenas for hot contests followed by rapine and bloodshed.

Q. Was there anything like this taught in ancient times: That God, for his own pleasure and glory, did, from all eternity, choose one portion (and that a very small number of men for heaven, and destined the rest to never-ending misery in hell, and that irrespective of anything done by them, whether good or evil? That is the belief of a great number of the Christian churches of the present day.

A. If your Christian churches believe that, they are worse than the idolators of my time; for even in the theology of Tyre, you will see that their Adonis (the Christ) teaches that all will ultimately be rescued from sin and misery.

Q. Did Jesus ever have any spiritual contact with mankind before his earthly (material) birth?

A. Yes; on certain rare occasions the heavenly messenger was the prince himself; for he who gave the law to Moses on Sinai was the same that came in due time to these Hebrews—who lived amongst them, but who was despised and crucified by them. He it was who stood as the ambassador of the great spirit on the mountain while it burned with sacred fire, and gave forth his laws or commandments to Moses. In some other portions of the Hebrew writings, he is spoken of as the angel of the lord.

Q. Did Joseph and Mary remain in Egypt after giving up Jesus to the care of Issha?

A. Yes; Joseph laboured at his craft, and both watched affectionately over Jesus when an infant. There was need for this care, for there, as elsewhere, there were many Hebrews who bore them no goodwill. But the priests exercised a watchful eye for their protection.

Q. As Arch Magus, did you preach what was afterwards known as the doctrines of Christ?

A. Even as Chief of the Magi, I had long held and taught these doctrines; and no one meddled with me until I proclaimed him from whom those doctrines came.

Q. Many of the battle stories etc in the Old Testament (Hebrew sacred writing seem greatly exaggerated and boastful—are they to be believed?

A. You may rely on the prophetic portions of the Hebrew records more than the historical. But the whole as handed down to your day, should be prized by you as embodying the most valuable records of spiritual sayings and doings of bygone times; and esteem them also as upholding the same theory of spirit communion which you (spiritualists) seek to advance.

Q. How were you provided with the means for undertaking your journeys?

A. I had been about twenty-six years in connection with the Magi, and had quite a sufficiency of funds whereby to undertake such travels. The Magi received support from the state, and also from the people as the teachers of youth, but of this I never took a penny. I required nothing. My possessions brought me in an ample yearly income for all my wants, and these were not many, for I was alone, and living was not high. And then I had neither soldiers nor vassals to feed; for when I became brother of the Magi, I gave away a portion of my possessions to my retainers, so that they might be able to maintain themselves, but with this condition—that, when called upon, they were to go forth to war. We had to carry our money with us of course, and we were frequently attacked by robber bands, thus for safety's sake we travelled as often as possible with caravans of merchants.

Q. Did you hold the doctrine of the atonement — that is, that Jesus, by his death on the cross, atoned for the sins of mankind?

A. At an after period of my life I held and preached doctrines somewhat similar to those held by Paul, but now I have changed my views of the doctrine in question. It is not alone by the death of Jesus, but by his whole life on earth, that man can be benefited, and by taking him as their great exemplar. If men would follow him — that is, love their fellows and love their God (for he did all that), then most assuredly, when they pass away from the mortal body, will they be admitted to the blest mansions of the just. I believe Paul would now tell you the same thing.

Q. Is it right in us to pray to Jesus?

A. Yes. In my day the followers of Jesus undoubtedly looked on him as their great medium of communication with God, and they reverently adored him. He is, indeed, the great king of kings, and reigneth in heaven and earth.

Q. Is Jesus cognisant of the communications you have made with us?

A. I can do nothing that is hid from him. In coming here, we are at perfect liberty. This is our mission, and if those who profess to be concerned for the prosperity of their churches would follow him, then would our visits be blessed to them, as they were blessed to the followers of the master in my day. Signs and wonders followed in the track of the humble teachers — the poor labourers and fishermen of Judea; the sick were healed, the blind received sight, the lame were made to walk, and evil spirits were driven out of poor mortals. And all this would again take place—spiritual power would again be put forth; but they bar their doors against us, and prefer to fight one with another for theological dogmas.

Q. Was it possible for Jesus, when in the body, to sin?

A. Yes, it was possible for him to fall; but I never could discover a fault in him. It is quite a possible thing to live a sinless life. From the time I last threw down the sword, I never sinned, neither against God, nor my brother, nor myself; I did whatever my conscience allowed me to do—whatever it told me was right. But, unlike others, I was greatly under spiritual influence, or guidance.

Q. Do you know of any record of the early churches in which your name is given?

A. If the records of the church in Persia were coming to light, you would find me mentioned therein; but the church was well nigh destroyed at my death.

Q. You spoke of your first interview with Paul in Athens, how long was it after the death of Christ?

A. It might have been eight or nine years; shortly after, I think, the beginning of the reign of Nero. The apostle was in Athens before that. It was a few years after the death of Jesus that Paul was converted. I do not think he had been in Rome when I first saw him.

Q. It is curious we have no mention in the four gospels of Jesus ever referring to his experiences in other countries which you have given?

A. He might have spoken of these for aught I know; but in his interviews with the Jews, it would have been unwise to refer to other nations to buttress up what he wished to impress on them, they were so bigoted a people. Hence, he would show them from their own sacred writings alone that his mission was from God. It would never have done to refer to such records as those of Persia or Egypt.

Q. Will you point out the difference between the teachings of the Magi and those of Jesus?

A. There was a great difference between the teachings; the latter spoke in a language so plain and simple that all men, the most unlearned, could understand; and his whole teachings were characterised by the great and gracious maxim—that men should love their fellow men as they love themselves. Though I, as one of the Magi had taught the same doctrine, my example was not generally followed by the brethren; on the contrary, it was common for them to enforce the doctrine that it was right to fight our enemies and do them all the hurt we could.

Q. Was Jesus born at the time of year we in the west celebrate it?

A. The proper date of the birth of Jesus was about the middle of your year, and about our harvest-time. The beginning of our year would be about two months before yours.

Q. Was the weekly sabbath observed by the Persians?

A. The Persians always held one day in seven as a sacred day. We were not like the nations around us, but more like the Hebrews in this, and many other things, so much so that I think they must have borrowed from us. In our little church our own meetings were daily, so every day was alike for us. In my day, the followers of Jesus, or 'Christians' as you call them, held the days that suited the country they were in; but there was no binding obligation to hold any particular day as a sabbath.

Q. *In one of the Epistles of Peter, the apostle, he says; 'The brethren in Babylon salute you.' Did you know of a church in Babylon?*

A. No, there was no such church in existence in my life-time; but he could not have been referring to the city of Babylon, for that in my day was but a heap of ruins, with a few miserable huts on the outskirts; possibly it was the district of country, or Babylonia that was meant.

Q. *Though you had passed away from the earth, might you not have known, as a spirit, of the existence of such a church, and of Peter's labours amongst them, seeing the district was so near to Persia?*

A. It was some time before I could get into communication with earth, I was so glad to be released—to meet with Jesus and the dear ones who had gone before, and to become one of the happy throng that walked in that great and glorious temple.

Q. *Will the consciousness of having done many things we ought not to have done, mar our happiness in the future life?*

A. Wilful wrong-doing, even though you return to God, must ever remain on your memory as a cause for regret. You would not be the same man could you forget your former life. But if you go on in sin—if you have not turned to God and goodness—suffer you must. Alas! How many are now howling in darkness because they have not returned to God!

Q. What is your opinion in regard to the doctrine commonly taught—that the death of Jesus was a satisfaction to God, by which He is enabled to remit the penalty due to the sins of all those who accept of Jesus as their substitute?

A. I do not wish to enter into that doctrine at present; I would only direct your attention to the fact that millions on millions of mankind never knew of Jesus and his doctrines. But are you to suppose that, because of their ignorance, they have been doomed to eternal despair? Jesus did not offer himself up as a sacrifice in the sense you speak of, but sinful men murdered him because of the grand and glorious principles which he incalculated. When the Christ came, the world was sunk in crime and darkness—so much was this the case that one would have thought the great God himself would require to do the work. But Jesus came. Did he come with a whip or a sword, and drive all before him? Ah, no; he came as a poor, meek, inoffensive man; so humble, he would not raise his voice; there was no ostentation with him, he displayed his love to all, and was ever ready to do a kindness to any one, even to his bitterest enemy. There was no pride, no Pharisaism to be seen in him; he lived the truths he taught. His heart went out in compassion for those who stood in need, and he gave what he had for the relief of rich and poor alike; while the hungry multitudes became receivers of his wondrous bounty. By a life-time of such deeds—a life in harmony with the words of wisdom that fell from his lips—he became the world's great exemplar, worthy to be followed by all men. He came to show

how to avoid the penalty—suffering; and that in loving his fellow-man, he best displayed his love of God.

Q. Are there now leaving the earth any fitted to enter into the paradise you have mentioned?

A. O yes; they enter there every day.

Q. You speak of little fishes sporting about the clear waters of the lakes in the vicinity of the great temple. Are these and the other animals there referred to of a spiritual nature?

A. They are spiritual, and yet have all the characteristics of the same tribes on earth.

Q. Have you, in your long experience of life in the spirit, ever met with an individual who had a remembrance of passing through more than one existence on earth?

A. No. If such were the case, I could not say I was myself. I believe I never was on the earth till I was sent direct from the great and mighty source of all spirit. Some men in the spirit world go back to earth, in the spirit, and teach the old doctrines they held in mortal life, and which they still tenaciously hold. Let such men come to stand on the same platform that I and others occupy, become frequenters of the great temple, and they will soon learn to think otherwise. Many of us, indeed, return to earth on errands of love and truth, but not in the body.

Q. Do you consider it hurtful for a medium to sit for physical, or lower manifestations?

A. In some cases it is hurtful. There are mediums adapted, by the peculiarity of their constitution, for these manifestations, and for no other. To such mediums, however, through whom very varied phenomena can be produced, mere physical manifestations become hurtful. The finer susceptibilities of such a medium get blunted or destroyed, and the animal portion of the medium is weakened by the withdrawal of the magnetism which he has received from the sun's rays; and not being possessed of a robust constitution, he (or she) is not open to the magnetism of the earth. But if the medium is strong, robust, he takes in that magnetism, which passes continually between the north and south poles, and also draws largely from the magnetism of those individuals who sit with him.

Q. You spoke of certain worlds you had visited whose inhabitants were 'all under the sway of one great head, and all are subject to the great king.' Am I right in understanding that each of these worlds is ruled by great heads, occupying the same relation to those worlds as Jesus does to ours?

A. No, you are not right in your supposition. What I meant to convey was this—that the worlds of the solar system, some of which are larger and some smaller than earth, have all their rulers, but all these are subordinate to the one great king—the prince. But we have also missions to worlds outside our system, who also have rulers or kings; and these are subject to him who is the king of kings, under the great and mighty spirit. Just as in Persia, in my day, the various chiefs or princes were under one king, so in these worlds referred to. These rulers may communicate with mortals on earth, just as Jesus does—that is, through a medium or mediums in the spirit world. I might be their medium. I might take a message to earth.

Q. *Is there anything differing in the personal appearance of the inhabitants of these other worlds you have visited from that of the inhabitants of this world?*

A. In shape they differ very little from the inhabitants of earth. They are more open in countenance, so that each one can read the character of his neighbour. In Saturn they are taller, and they live to a greater age, being much more robust than the inhabitants of earth.

Q. *Are the inhabitants of such worlds acquainted with the state or condition of this world?*

A. Yes; they are, to some extent, acquainted with the affairs of earth through information derived from those who have left your world. Constituted as you are on earth, they are possessed of the same desires to attain to something higher; and consequently we find them seeking after knowledge—praying into the heavens as you do, to learn something of the worlds rolling in space around them, and anxious, like the philosophers of earth, to discover the laws which govern those wonderful and glorious works of the Almighty's hand. But they are in a much higher condition for receiving and imparting instruction than the inhabitants of earth. I knew comparatively little of those great bodies that have attracted the attention of astronomers in all ages of your world. But still, I think, we of the Magi were as far advanced in our ideas of the nature of the heavenly bodies as your philosophers of the present day, (1872).

Q. *Were you aware of the earth turning on its axis?*

A. A few of us were. In Rome, Greece, and Egypt there were controversies amongst the learned on this subject—some contending for the globular form, and others maintaining that it was flat. There was a similar diversity of opinion amongst the

Hebrews. In Persia there were great disputes on this point; and each section of the Magi had its own theories. In my own circle, we knew and believed that the earth turned on its axis from certain signs which came under our observation.

Q. Do you know if the earth (as some say) is a hollow globe, inhabited, and open at the Poles?

A. The earth is hollow, but not at all fitted for habitation. But I do not believe it is open at both Poles.

Q. Did you, when on earth, know of a doctrine held by some—namely, that the body of Jesus was not a human body, but one similar to those in which spirits are making themselves visible to mortal sight?

A. I never heard of such a doctrine in my day. Jesus had a body such as you have. He felt as you feel: he had all the feelings peculiar to humanity. Had it been made up only for the time being, those who hold such a doctrine have got to explain how it was left hanging on the cross, and not dissolved when the spirit left it. But, doubtless it underwent some chemical change in the tomb. Your sacred books say it saw no corruption, and that statement is assuredly correct. That same body that hung on the cross he used when he appeared to his followers. He needed to appear in such a body as that referred to by you: he was so spiritual in character, that he possessed, even in his human form, almost all the powers of a disembodied spirit. Then again, as evidence to some that doubted, he showed them the wounds in his body, proving that it was the same body that had been nailed to the cross. They needed to be confirmed in all that they, as disciples, had seen and heard, so that they might be fully armed in going forth on their mission to the world. We know, however, that his earthly body was dissolved in the act of ascension.

Q. Do you suppose it likely that a person could be carried by spirits from one place to another?

A. Yes; spirits are able to do so. They can bring a stone through a solid wall, and they can, in the same way, bring a living body.

Q. A friend has told me that the spirit of his son remarked recently that he had travelled four hundred miles in three minutes. Can you tell me anything as to the speed of spirits in going from one place to another?

A. In the case of your friend's son it might have taken that time; in others it is different. Those who are fully developed, who have been long in spirit-life, travel as quick as thought.

Q. Do different societies in the spirit world wear costumes of various colours?

A. Yes; but white prevails. I have always worn white, which was my habit on earth. I wore a chaplet when Head of the Magi, and I wear one still; indeed, I still wear sandals, and I am still girt about with a girdle.

Q. Do the spirits appear to you in spirit-life as they appear to mortal eye on earth?

A. Yes; we perceive a black man as such, and we see a fair man as such. But better far, we are able to perceive each others character; hence no wolf need come here in sheep's clothing. Indeed, they would not abide with us—our pursuits would not suit them. A righteous man, loving his fellow-man as he does himself, leaving the body, enters here in an elevated state. There is no change in his character. An unjust man enters the spirit-life—he may have been a robber; here, however, though unchanged in character, he cannot rob, but he may combine with other spirits to influence earthly man to rob. They band themselves together in these dark regions (dark to them, but beautiful to us) to carry out their wicked schemes, prolonging their misery and wretchedness—but there is even hope for them. But the solitary ones are in a worse state. They wander about in their dark and gloomy course, without hope, cursing, despairing, and lamenting their unhappy lot—thinking they are abandoned both by God and man. But they are not forgotten. We are ever striving to get them to open their eyes to the truth. At last they begin to see, and then it is we can do something to bring them up to the light of truth.

Q. Why are some mediums so much better than others?

A. Some mediums have great difficulties to contend with in their development; and we too find many obstacles in our way which cannot be easily overcome, but which in time gradually melt away. I observe that there is a disposition on the part of some people to find fault with mediums. This is not right. What is a medium? He is merely an instrument to be played on by the controlling spirit—a tool with which he works. How little will destroy the true sound of a musical instrument, and in such a case you will get nothing but discord, even from the most expert player. Even so the indisposition of the medium damages that which comes through him. Though you get a communication bearing on its face a direct contradiction, do not be ready to blame either the spirit controlling, or the poor medium who is controlled. Be charitable in your verdict concerning both. True spirits are often shamefully used by the ignorant and thoughtless, frustrated in every way by the antagonistic condition and frivolity of the so-called investigators. Beware of this. On the other hand, mediums should never get proud of their powers as mediums. The world may say they are gifted, and so they are, but let them ever bear in mind that the gift may be withdrawn at any moment. Mediums should ever be wary of the company they keep, from bad company may come bad spirits since a medium is so open to influence. Especially is the case with the vain or conceited medium, who is often unconsciously used by such spirits to say and do things of a deceptive character, which when found out, damage his reputation, and hurt him in every way.

Q. Is it the case that the spirit of man retires from the body in sleep, and enters into another conscious state of existence?

A. Yes; such is the case. That question and others of the same nature formed the subject of my study in leisure hours when on earth. It is one worth studying. Look at a man in deep sleep. Half an hour before, he was a strong, active man, one you would not willingly encounter as an enemy. Stretched on his bed in sleep, what is he? While sleeping, you have no fear of him; though he were your greatest foe, he has now no power to harm you; his strength is gone; his limbs are as powerless as are a babe's; his powers of reasoning, thinking, or acting, have vanished. The body rests. But the spirit sleeps not. After the day's toil—say he is a hard-working man (and that may be either in bodily or mental labour), worn out by fatigue, the spirit as well as the body must have rest, else he could not go on with his daily duties. So, when the body is laid to rest, exhausted by the labours of the day, it goes forth into the spirit-life: that is its rest. Observe the effects of change of scene in your own earth experience: both body and mind receive that relaxation so needful to the well-being of every human being.

Q. Is the spirit in a state of consciousness capable of receiving instruction, while absent from the body?

A. Oh, yes; the spirit is conscious while the body sleeps; but on coming back, on the waking up of the body, the conjunct being has but a dreamy, confused perception of anything that has taken place. Some dream that they have seen faces of friends and others whom they know have passed away long long ago. Oftentimes, places and circumstances belonging to the days of childhood and youth will be brought up in panoramic vision, in which the faces and forms of the long lost appear as in active life. But there are dreams that are only caused by the derangement of the bodily system. The true spiritual dream—that which is caused by the separate action of the spirit—will, on the waking up of the body, fade away in a minute; something may, however, bring up the circumstances afresh to memory, for they are printed there, though lost for the time being.

Q. *Have the inhabitants of other worlds material bodies like ours, and do they pass away like us into their several spirit worlds?*

A. I thought I had already spoken on this subject. I told you that in those worlds with which I am acquainted, there is nothing of that which you experience as death. In many cases in your own world, death is accompanied with great pain and suffering of both body and mind. But in the worlds referred to, it is very different. In these happy worlds, the inhabitants live to a great age; having run their course, they go, as it were to sleep and awaken in the spirit world invested with the spirit body. It is not, you will perceive, *your* death, but a translation. All have material bodies, and all in due time pass quietly away into the spirit world, which is the great universe. I know of no spirit sphere (as you call it) belonging to one world and not to another. Although spirits from worlds outside the solar system do not generally intermingle with those spirits belonging to it, there is nothing absolutely to prevent them. I may illustrate this by directing your attention to that which you see on earth. Spread over the surface of the earth, you have many countries in varied forms, sizes, and features; these, again, peopled by different races, with many languages, manners, customs, and religions—all differing, yet all belonging to the earth: and these tribes of men are all drawn to their respective localities by the ties that bind mankind generally—that is, by sympathy in nationality, religion etc, even so is it in the spirit state. There still prevails a feeling of kinship by which the spirits of one nation are drawn towards those who have gone before, who belonged to that nation. The peoples of the earth have their localities here as they had while sojourning in the mortal body; but there is nothing to hinder those outside our system inter-mixing with us, any more than there is anything to prevent natives of one country on earth mingling with those of another.

Q. *Is it the case that those who have lived most in harmony with the laws of God find it easier to take on spirit form?*

A. Yes it certainly is. But, notwithstanding, such a one may suffer greatly before he is able to quit the mortal body. His fore-fathers may have been transgressors, and not only have suf-fered themselves, but sown the seeds of misery for future generations. As the Hebrew record has it, the sins of the fathers fall on the children to the third and fourth generations and even farther. They must suffer the father's sins; it cannot be avoided. How different in those other planets where sin is not known! There the golden age still exists. There you will find no gloomy anticipation of death as on earth, but all are happy in contemplating the change from the mortal to the immortal; for so keen and clear is their spiritual vision—so pure and lovely are they in their lives, that they see the spirits of their departed friends, and these see the human form, and have intimate communion the one with the other, walking and talking in loving friendship.

Q. *Are all worlds in this happy condition?*

A. No; there have been worlds, in long past ages, the dwellers on which were far greater transgressors than the inhabitants of the earth. They were so much opposed to the laws of the great and almighty spirit—so very wicked, that they and the worlds they inhabited were swept to destruction: yet those sinners, once so vile in their rebellion in the ages of the past, are now, I know, amongst the brightest angels that walk the heavenly courts.

Q. *There is a statement in the mosaic record, that 'Enoch walked with God, and God took him.' Do you know if he died, or was he translated (as is commonly taught) without tasting death?*

A. That case as recorded is just an illustration of what I was speaking of—I mean the passing away of mortals in the unfallen worlds. You will find the case recorded in our Persian books too; for Enoch was a Chaldean. There have been many holy men whose lives are recorded in the sacred books of all nations, and Enoch may be taken as a sample of the whole. Indeed, I have seen those who worshipped graven images, of whom it might truly be said, 'They walked with God, and God took them.'

Q. *Jesus, according to your statement, is the head or anointed one of the solar worlds. Have these worlds had a revelation of him similar to that which has been made to us?*

A. Not exactly. The inhabitants of these worlds cannot be blamed as the murderer of their prince. They acknowledge him as their king. He has visited these worlds in the same manner as he visited earth before his advent as a man. He has appeared to them as their lord. Not many know of his mission to earth; indeed, it is seldom taken notice of. I myself, though his friend and companion on earth, must nevertheless be classed as one of his murderers; for, though I maintained a blameless life, I often felt that I still was subject in some degree to the 'old man'—in other words, that I was one of earth's children. Would I have denied my lord? No! Still I was but human.

Q. Has the Christian system in ages past been the best one as an agent in man's elevation?

A. The religion of Jesus was not a system in itself; it drew from all the other systems. He rejected that which was evil, and took that which was good in the prevailing systems, and taught it to his followers. Had they walked in his footsteps, their course would have been glorious; for then their progress, like his, would have been accompanied by many wonderful works, to convince those who were opposed to the truth which they sought to propagate.

Q. It is stated in the Hebrew records that on Moses coming down from the mountain, and finding the Israelites engaged in the worship of golden calf, he led on a general massacre, in which thirty thousand persons were slain. Do you consider that, in so doing, he was acting in harmony with the will or law of God?

A. Oh no, no! God never brought war and bloodshed on mankind, and never will. The high and holy one never instructed man to slay his fellow-man. Had Moses but reflected on the story of Cain and Abel, which he himself gives, he would have seen that, at the very outset—from the beginning, God reprobates the shedding of man's blood: there we find that the murderer was not slain, but, with a stamp on him, he felt himself driven out from his fellow-men—out from the God whose law he had broken—as a wanderer on earth's surface, to repent in bitterness the ruthless deed. But Moses was terribly provoked, and, in his anger, he forgot that which he should have remembered. He did a deed that day for which I am sure he is now deeply sorry: and should I meet him, I have no doubt he would acknowledge he had done wrong. I, too, feel deeply grieved on reflecting on some actions of my earth-life; had I my life to live again, such actions would be avoided by me. Think not that the sins and follies of the bodily life are forgiven, that they ever can be forgotten by those who committed them.

Q. *Is music produced in the same way with you as with us—that is, by the vibration of the atmosphere?*

A. Yes; and by both instruments and voice.

Q. *Why do you and Paul abide so long in your present sphere?*

A. Were Paul and I to go to a higher place, we should find ourselves idle—the blessed work in which we have so long been labouring would be at an end. Remember, we both feel deeply the obligation to work. Neither Paul nor I are tired of the work. Our great delight is to throw in the light upon our brethren of mankind who still stand in opposition to God. We still wish to lift them up, and bring them into the presence of Jesus the prince.

Q. *Is it possible for a spirit to give manifestations without the presence of what we term a medium?*

A. It is quite possible; but a medium must have been in the place before, and left some of his influence or magnetism there; otherwise the spirit could not act. The spirit may act without the knowledge of the medium, but the medium must have been there.

Q. *Is there in the spirit world a sun, similar to that of our system, doing the same work for you as ours does for us?*

A. No, we require it not. We have continuous light emanating from the great source of all light, and by which the orbs are supplied. Were we to get our light from a sun, we should, like you on earth, have night and day. The light we have is so pure, and of such a nature, that I cannot find words to explain it to you. The medium sees it, but it is not the same to his vision as to ours.

Q. *Did the Jews, in your day, hold the doctrine of what is called the trinity—that is, three persons in the Godhead, equal in power and glory?*

A. Like other eastern nations in my day, the Hebrews held a trinity in God, not exactly as you have put it. They believed in the great father, the one source of all being. But the second, the son, was wisdom; and the holy spirit, or Michael. The winged figure over the sacred ark was doubtless the Goddess Isis, borrowed from Egypt. The great spirit was, by the nations of the east, looked at under three aspects, and these in course of time took form as persons. In some nations they had a fourth, a rebel spirit. Of course I now look at the subject under a different light. There was some measure of truth in all these early conceptions of God; for I most emphatically maintain, whether you believe it or not, that there is a trinity of everything, and there is a trinity in God, who is theme and only source of all being, wherever manifested, spiritual and material; and that every one of us—the race of man—is part and parcel of Him. All spring from the great and the mighty one—not from three; there cannot be three Gods equal in power. Jesus, though filled to overflowing with the holy spirit, was the offspring of God, and such are all men. There have been others who manifested a great amount of godlike character, insomuch that their fellow-men in some cases termed them gods; but none of the men could at all be compared with Jesus. Some of these, it has been said, could even raise the dead; but he my prince, could do all that he desired to do—he had but to say the word and the work was done. He was and is greater than all.

Q. *Had our lord while on earth, correct ideas of things hidden from men of science at that time, such as the existence of unknown continent?*

A. O yes; we discourse about these matters when on our travels. He knew of other peoples and places, unknown to other men. This I could not doubt, for we were told by spirits who communicated with us that they had been on various unknown parts of the earth.

Q. *Had you in Persia, anything else than wood for fuel, or was the mineral called coal in use among eastern nations?*

A. We had that which you call coal, but it was scarce, and generally obtained when digging for iron. The land being well cultivated, our forests were not so extensive as those of some other countries, and consequently we had to import our fuel from neighbouring nations.

Q. *Have you any knowledge of the mechanical power by which the huge stones of the pyramids, and of the temples in the east were raised?*

A. In regard to the rearing of the pyramids, I have no knowledge, nor has anyone else. But the great masses of stone used in the building of the celebrated temples were put up in their places by means of a gin, to the long spokes of which were harnessed horses, camels, and elephants. They also used a great lever in their operations. It is likely the pyramids were erected in the same way.

Q. Were there any approaches made in the olden time to the art of printing—that is, the mode of taking impressions from raised types of letters and words?

A. Yes, we, the Magi, had some knowledge of the process. This was first of all received from some of our former brethren who had travelled in the far east. Zoroaster, it was said by some, brought back on his return from his travels, a knowledge of this art. On certain occasions we used sheets of copper, lead or silver, on which we scratched out the words with a steel pen. The plate was then coated with a back dye, and we took impressions on fine parchment by rubbing. This was done only when we wanted to preserve that which was written. When we wrote on parchment, we used a vegetable dye.

Q. Have the spirits the power to do the works which Jesus did, as these are recorded in what we term the gospels—such as causing the storm to cease?

A. Yes; spirits of a higher order have great power. Water is agitated by under currents and atmospheric changes—it must be agitated; the law is constantly at work—when not in an agitated state, water becomes impure, corrupt, stagnant. But when strong winds prevail, caused by a vacuum in the atmosphere, you have your hurricanes or tempests, which sweep across the sea and land, destroying in their course your largest ships, tearing up trees by the roots, and devastating the dwellings of man. In the case referred to by you, it must be remembered that Jesus had this spirit power in full measure. He was master of the elements above and below. But even great as was the power wielded by him, the day will come, when those who can be used amongst mortals, will be used by us not only to subdue the tempest in its desolating track, but to prevent its uprising; and by thus holding the elements in hand, they will become the instruments of saving many lives, and preserving much property on sea and land.

Q. We have some difficulty in understanding why some spirits should appear in an aged form, such as you appear in, and others in all the strength and beauty of manhood.

A. I still appear in the form I last had on earth. There is nothing compulsory in this; we are not forced to assume such forms. But is the appearance of old age not as beautiful as that of youth?

Q. That is not exactly what I am referring to. I allude to decrepitude which is often seen in old age.

A. The spirit is not decrepit. The mortal body may be, and often is, before the spirit leaves; but the spirit is straight as an arrow. Many poor spirits are imprisoned in mortal bodies, where they are cramped, and cannot work; but, once quit of their bodies, they are all right. They are at liberty—free! Take the case of an idiot. You may imagine, in your ignorance, that the spirit in such circumstances remains undeveloped. It is not so. It has gained a thousand times greater experience than many who are in possession of all their senses, and has become fit to dwell with saints, not with devils. And so it is with the aged. The body may be weak, deformed, deprived of hearing, sight, or feeling; but these defects are left behind—they all pass off by what you call death.

Q. I often think of the multitudes who appear to have no control over the circumstances in which they are placed. Does it not look like ordination or destiny on the part of God?

A. If born a savage, the man has no control over that; but we cannot blame the creator in this. When man first appeared, be the time when it may, God's law was that he was to come on earth in the same way as other animals came—by procreation. Conception takes place, and a spirit must be in that body. There are no circumstances in which a man is placed but can, to some extent, be controlled by him so as to better himself. Here is one for example, born in a depraved community. As a spirit, he is in a very low condition, but a far higher, nobler condition than that of the brute. He knows when he is doing wrong, and when he is doing righteously. But he goes on in the evil courses of such a community, he heeds not the inner voice warning him, checking him in his evil ways; and he becomes hardened in his iniquity. He knows he may live a better life, and that there is room on the globe for him—that he is free to leave the society of the evil, and mingle with the good, but yet he cares not. Still, you will find, even amongst such men, some true, good principles, significant of something better than what appears; and I have known some of these, on leaving the body, become bright characters in the spirit world. Your question is not a new one. It formed the subject of disputation, before my day, amongst the Greeks.

Q. *Does the body of man receive a portion of the almighty spirit?*

A. The body of man is made up from the elements of the material world, the spirit from those of the spiritual world; while the soul, the inner man, is the offspring of the spirit world of which none of us—no, not even the blessed ones who are nearest to Him—know anything. We do know something of the other parts, but of that part of man we know nothing. You see your own body; we see our spirit bodies, but we cannot see our souls—*ourselves.*

Q. *At what time does the spirit portion become connected with the body?*

A. I can only give you my opinion, for it is still a subject of discussion in our spiritual halls. After the germ in the womb becomes developed in shape—after it has become not many inches in size, and formed as a body, the spirit-body begins also its growth with the material body; but not until life is felt can it be said that the soul has taken up its abode in the spirit-body. Yet it may never live to breathe. The blood does not circulate in the unborn body as it does in life out of the womb. You are not to suppose that the blood is the life, it is but the supporter of life, and it is not requisite while the child is still in the womb. Many children, alive in the womb, are born into death. They never breathe your atmosphere. Why? Because the thin membrane which covers the mouths of the heart valves remain unbroken by the action of the atmospheric air; when this thin covering is snapped the child lives and breathes, becomes a denizen of earth; when it is not rent, the child goes to the better world.

Q. *Is 'sphere' a right term to use when we wish to speak of a place in the spirit world?*

A. It does not much matter what term you use, so that it is understood. Doubtless it does well enough when used for the word place. The heavens are like a vast plain, on which are to be found all grades and conditions of spirits. Hell and heaven are at no great distance from each other. In the one they wander in gloomy darkness, while in the other, the happy spirits flit about in glory.

Q. How is it that, in the case of this medium, when he sits down, we find that the spirit is here, ever ready to control him, giving us the idea that other duties do not press very hard on your attention?

A. As I have just said, we know of your intended meetings before-hand, even though these should appear to be by mere accident, and we make arrangements whereby we can come to you. Though dwellers and workers in the higher heavens, we do not think God's footstool too low for us to sit on. Earth, in our eyes, is as grand as the brightest centre of heaven; so do not imagine we are restrained from coming to you, it is just part of our duty. When the thought is materialised that you are to meet, we make ready to meet you.

Q. Are your efforts to reclaim the fallen in the spirit world confined to such as the Great Xerxes—that is, to prominent men only?

A. Oh no, no. What could ever tempt you to put such a question? What! Give our attention to the salvation of those only who, while on earth, had been the occupants of thrones, arrayed in all the luxurious splendour of royalty? Oh, no! The meanest and most wretched beggar that has wearily paced the highway, or has sat on the wayside, a miserable, helpless cripple, in rags and in loathsomeness, is equal, in the sight of God, with him who has been one of the world's crowned monarchs. There is no difference in our eyes; all are the objects of our care and compassion.

Q. Are there many besides you who choose to remain in their present sphere or condition, for the purpose of benefiting the fallen ones?

A. In my condition, or sphere, all are missionaries; and the innumerable host of spirits (innumerable to you, not us) from every nation of the earth, and even from other worlds, are all actively and willingly employed in the up-raising of those below them.

Q. *Is it possible for spirits in low condition to gratify the animal appetites they acquired on earth?*

A. No, no; were such the case there would be no punishment. If the spirit had been one addicted to drunkenness when on earth, and got what he desired of wine in the spirit world, he would be content—he would not be likely to leave such a sphere; he would then be comparatively happy.

Q. *Can low-conditioned spirits come back to earth?*

A. Those who are in the lowest condition—the solitary and wretched wanderers of the dark caverns—are prisoners, and cannot get back so long as they are in that state: a state different from that of those spirits who do come back, who are in what is called the second sphere, whom upraising influences have been powerless to carry beyond that state. The spirits in this sphere band themselves together for the purpose of working out their malicious and disorderly schemes through the instrumentality of spirits in the body; and many of the blackest deeds of mischief done by men are first hatched by these devils in that low sphere, who alas, never lack fitting instruments to execute the work on earth. Depend upon it, they are at the bottom of much of the misery and wickedness existing on earth. You know that one great feature in the earth mission of Jesus was the driving out of these spirits from the poor mortals who were controlled by them.

Q. Why do Red Indians form such a large proportion of the spirit guides who come through to us on the earth?

A. They are truly a noble race of men; the children of nature, and taught by nature, they become more open to spiritual influence, even in earth-life, more than other men. Their elevation takes but a short time when they enter the spirit world, and they are generally found in what is called the third sphere—a state beyond that of the mischief-makers; and even in the case of a few Indians who are found in the second sphere or condition, we find that they are much more easily induced to depart from it to a higher state than others. In seeking to raise them, we find that they have little to learn, compared with what the white man has to acquire—rather, I should say, has to unlearn.

Q. Have the spirits of the second sphere, who, as you say are banded together, busily engaged hatching evil deeds, any degree of pleasure or happiness enticing them to remain in that state?

A. Yes; the spirits of the second sphere are those who, when in the body, had pleasure in wickedness. As spirits they remain in the same state. With perfect freedom to return, they have, alas, through the medium of mankind, too many opportunities of indulging their lawless appetites and passions, deriving thereby as much pleasure as when they were in the body: and not only so, but they find delight in enticing mankind to mischief and disorder, bringing in their train misery and ruin to the guilty and innocent alike. Such unholy deeds have for ages been ascribed to one grand potentate of evil, termed the devil; but it is not so: these denizens of what is called the second sphere are the devils.

Q. Understanding you and other of our friends occupy what we call the sixth sphere—a condition, as we have been told, of happiness, light, and love—will you favour us with some account of the character and pursuits of the dwellers in the third, fourth, and fifth spheres, taking them up one by one?

A. Yes; I have already said that when we were successful in leading a spirit past or beyond the second sphere, we were sure of him—getting into the third state or sphere, he was in comparative safety—he had got outside the line of evil. In the third sphere, there is a certain amount of real happiness, varying according to the state of the individual, morally and intellectually, and this also is characteristic of the higher spheres. It is in this third sphere that a change begins to be seen, and gradually the spiritual vision is opened; then come, now and again, glimpses of the, as yet, far off land of the sixth sphere and its gloriously beautiful temple; all things in nature begin to look grander, more worthy of admiration, and to afford pleasure never before experienced: and as the spirit thus develops in strength, there is a corresponding development in his appreciation of everything by which he is surrounded. With his spiritual vision ever increasing in strength, the spirit at length begins to enjoy the society of visitors from the other and higher spheres—the brighter and better regions of the spirit world. With such he meets, and through the happy intercourse, he is led to press on and on, from one degree of goodness to another—ever onward, till he reaches the great centre—beyond this sixth sphere, out far into the great ocean of bliss.

Q. Are we right in speaking of the spirit spheres as places or localities, separated by distance, and higher and lower?

A. Yes; I have, I think, spoken of this before. It is difficult to convey the idea; but I will try. Take, for example, the earth which, as compared with other bodies revolving in space, is but a grain of sand—well then, take this globe of yours, and look on it as a great flat plain; for *you* do not look on it as a round body: over that plain you have spread various countries; India, Ethiopia, Persia, Greece—in every degree of latitude; and according to the position they occupy in relation to the sun's rays, so is their appearance. Here you have on the one hand districts which are cold and dreary, rugged and barren; on the other, perpetual summer, and the most luxuriant vegetation; while between these two extremes there are many countries possessed of climates well adapted for man's development in physical and intellectual vigour. Even so is it in the spirit world; each part of the whole is adapted to the varied states or conditions. But the spirit is not always confined to one part; as he advances in condition, so does he pass from one part to another adapted to his condition.

Q. Then how does that correspond with the oft repeated statement; that, in spirit, space is annihilated?

A. It matters not whether you view space from the mortal or from the spiritual stand-point, it remains the same. You propose to go on a journey, and you calculate the distance and the time you will take to accomplish the journey; but in our case the flight is so rapid, quick as thought, that we may well say time and space are annihilated; the space is there nevertheless.

Q. Are there in the spheres mentioned, conclaves of artists, philosophers, theologians, astronomers etc—that is, do they come together because of intellectual sympathies, or from moral obligations?

A. It is only on this sphere that such assemblages as you refer to take place, and that within the great temple. In the lower states of the spirit world, they begin to draw together, and have their meetings, but not to the same extent; all, however, are pressing onward, striving after higher and still higher attainments.

Q. Was the doctrine of the trinity, held by the great majority of Christian churches, derived originally from the Egyptian theology, and Freemasonry?

A. I at once say, that the doctrine of the trinity is truth. Why, you will find that there is a trinity in everything; in man, in animals, in everything scattered over the field of nature, you will find a trinity. All the nations of the east believed in God as a trinity; they might indeed have had their gods many, but they had always the idea of the one great and good being manifested in three different aspects.

Q. The natural (material) body is constantly throwing off particles of the old frame and forming new. Is there a similar operation going on in respect to the spiritual body?

A. Yes; as the spirit rises from one condition to another, he casts off the old and takes on the new: the operation is always going on through all the spheres, and when he reaches this sphere—this higher condition, it still goes on. It is the same in all the workings of nature. She is ever, by throwing off waste, purifying herself; and so the great work goes on throughout all her kingdoms—there is no exception. Nature has within herself the power to sustain herself.

Q. Do our departed friends know the time of our approaching death, and do they await us on the other side?

A. It will very much depend on the condition of those friends. If advanced, they will know when death approaches: oftentimes when conditions are favourable, they can and do prevent premature death by accident. But when the individual has reached the natural term of earth-life, then they stand by waiting, ready to receive you in spirit, and bear you to the place adapted for you; so that when you awake to consciousness, your eyes at once look on the faces of the loved ones that passed on before. But if evil in condition, the unhappy spirit will inevitably fall into the hands of those on the other side who are like-minded.

Q. Are the grotesque and hideous figures of objects seen by men in delirium-tremens real or imaginary?

A. Those who drink wine to the extent of stealing away reason, or destroying the proper action of that organ of the brain by which the spirit works, are subject to all the consequences of the wrong done to the organ. They see these frightful scenes and figures, and imagine them to be realities; they are however, only the effects from a deranged and outraged brain. There is nothing real in anything seen by the poor drunkard while in this condition.

Q. It has been stated by those who believe in reincarnation, that there is no such thing as sex in the spirit world. Is that the case?

A. No such thing as sex! The man is still the man—the woman is still the woman in spirit-life. We do not lose our identity.

Q. It has been said that murderers, suicides, and such like, haunt the places in which they have perpetrated their evil deeds, unable to get quit of earth. What do you say to this?

A. The murderer and suicide are not permitted to return. But in cases of murder done in secret, the spirit of the victim is often permitted to wander near the scene of the murder, so as to attract the attention of the living (I mean by that those who are still in the body), and thus lead to the discovery of the murderer. And there have been cases where good, living men and women who, having been fully deprived of life, have been enabled, through proper mediums, to show a vision of the deed; the place where the murder was perpetrated; the murderer himself; the secret place where the body lay; and when the criminal was at length brought to justice, the spirit would no longer hover about, but gladly leave for its home in the spirit world. But generally the spirits which haunt certain places are of a somewhat low standing or character.

Q. Do you know whether there are any other revelations which have been made through mediums in regard to the life and character of Jesus?

A. I know not. Paul may have came back for such a purpose; but I rather think not, for he himself only knew of these things by hearsay. As regards the early part of the life of Jesus, very few in Judea knew anything about it—that part being spent principally in Egypt and Persia. On his return to Judea his life was, for a few years, one of seclusion; for, being the inhabitant of a small, obscure village or town, he would only be known to a few immediate friends. Subsequently, on his second visit to Persia, he began to attract public attention, by the exercise of the great gifts with which he was endowed, as I have already mentioned. But coming out as a public teacher in his own land, his sayings, and doings for the three years of his ministry had all to be recorded—though it must be confessed, you have but a meagre summary of the whole. The Jews, if they chose, could give you much more than you already have in what you call the gospels.

Q. How is it that, when we have letters and narratives left us by several of the followers of Jesus, we have nothing extant from his own pen?

A. Oh, I think the reason is simple. During the three years of his public career as a teacher, he was always attended by a few followers; and to these he required not to write, they never being far from him—never scattered abroad, as they afterwards were: all that was necessary for them to know was given by words which fell from his lips. Had he lived longer on earth, and his followers been spread in course of time over various countries, letters would have assuredly been written by him to them. But, another reason why you have no writings of Jesus may be, that he did not wish the Jewish doctors an opportunity of gratifying their passion for controversy and wrangling. The letters he did write during these years were sent to Egypt and Persia.

Q. *Is there anything in spirit-life corresponding to our trade and commerce?*

A. No, no; where such is carried on evil must exist. There is nothing having a tendency to evil permitted where I am. What could we trade in? I have no lands—no goods which I can call my own. All is free to me as it is to you. There is no such thing as personal property here.

Q. *Would you now express to us the value or importance of prayer?*

A. That I will gladly do. We must meanwhile leave it over; for the subject is one so grand, so important, in every aspect, both for man and spirit, that it cannot be passed over with a few words; it must be dwelt with at some length. It is one of those subjects on which I delight to dwell! O great indeed is the privilege conferred on man—on bended knee, to lift up his supplicating eyes upwards to the great father of spirits. When your children look up to you and prattle forth their little wants, you do not—you cannot close your ears. Neither will your father and ours withhold his answer to our prayers and yours. As sure as He sends His high and holy ones to us with an answer to our supplications, so surely does He answer your prayers by sending us to you in ways you think not of. Go, then, with humble heart and bended knee, with uplifted hands and eyes—go with heart following eye, to Him who is the source of all good—present the desires of your soul, and He, the hearer of prayer, will assuredly answer. I loved, when on earth, to retire at times to a sequested spot in the shady grove, where a little streamlet ran rippling over its pebbly bed, with no living soul to disturb my meditations, and there my soul held sweet communion—there I talked with the great and mighty spirit.

Q. Do spirits exercise a choice of dress or costume in spirit-life?

A. In manifesting our presence to mortals, we appear in the dress we should best be known by. I appear in the costume I used when head of the Magi. Ancient philosophers would appear in the robes usually worn by them in the earth-life. Indeed, to appear in true spirit-form and dress would be useless; the medium would not know us. The colour of the clothing of the spirit is white, indicating purity. All the spirits in this particular sphere are so clothed; while those in lower spheres are clothed according to moral condition: as is the state, so is the clothing.

Q. Are you subject in the spheres to atmospheric phenomena, such as cold, heat, rain, or snow?

A. No, no! I have already explained that spheres, as you call them, are conditions or states. We have nothing of that nature to disturb us. We require no rain to produce vegetation, for that is not the kind of sustenance needed. The vegetation here is not developed in the same way as that of the material worlds.

Q. If there is no rain, how do you get the flowing rivers?

A. The clouds floating in our skies resemble the clouds of the earth, in so far as they give variety to the scene, and relieve the eye, which would weary were it otherwise, but they give no rain. We have rivers, seas, lakes; when and how these came to be is as much a mystery to me as it is to you.

Q. Are the animals in the spirit-world wild, ferocious in their nature?

A. No, no! There is nothing wild or ferocious here; all is harmony. We have lions, tigers, and other wild animals, as you would call them, but in nature they are like the lamb. Men, women, and children may play with them, and no harm be done—all is love, peace, and happiness. It cannot be otherwise. Our animal passions no longer exist here—there are no longer in us feelings of discord and war—nothing of that sort; and these animals live, as we live, in harmony with existing spiritual conditions. It would not do to cut off the lower tribes from spirit-life, for without these man is incomplete. As I have said before, you will find that man embodies all the lower orders of creation.

Q. You have more than once said your acquaintance with the four gospels depended on the medium's knowledge of them. Could you not get information from some of the disciples of Jesus, or from the writers of the gospels?

A. O yes, that I could; but I never took thought about these gospels, or the writings of his followers. It is much easier, and certainly far better, for me to get it from Jesus himself.

Q. *What provision is made for the ignorant but morally fit spirit who enters your sphere, so as to raise him intellectually?*

A. There are thousands waiting ready to take such a one by the hand. Why, you know well, they are not to blame for their lack of knowledge; they have been neglected, it may be, in their earth-life, but there are those here who will not neglect to impart the knowledge they require. Sitting like little children, they will in due time, under their loving teachers, become like the greatest philosophers, if not the oldest.

Q. *Can spirits see material objects as we see them?*

A. Yes; if these objects come within certain spiritual conditions. We perceive all material things through the spiritual atmosphere, or aura, surrounding them. We do not see a human being in bodily form—we see him as a spirit; but in coming into *rapport* with an individual, we do perceive him in his material form. There are some, however, with whom we cannot harmonise—that is to say, the currents flowing from spirit to man, and from man to spirit, do not harmonise; therefore we cannot perceive them. *The spirit body is also material,* but of such a fine nature that it cannot, under ordinary conditions, be perceived by *your* bodily eyes; and it is the same with our perception of the material body—the spirit cannot, under certain conditions, see the body.

Q. *When spirits converse with each other, do they produce sounds by the use of vocal organs?*

A. Oh, yes; we can speak as you speak, but our speech is quite of a different character—certainly much more refined—spiritual; so much so, indeed, that we cannot use it on earth. Again, we can read the thoughts of spirits, and under certain conditions the thoughts of spirits in the body: we know indeed what a spirit is about to say.

Q. Is it right to think of God, who is everywhere present, as a person located in heaven, such as we have in the Lord's Prayer *'Our Father which art in Heaven'?*

A. I will reply to that question with my answer to another: Where is heaven? Universal creation is heaven. The earth which you now inhabit, even to its very central depths, is heaven. Each planet, as it rolls on in majesty throughout the grand ocean of space, is heaven. Everywhere—wherever God is—there is heaven.

Q. But you have yourself spoken of coming into 'the immediate presence of God,' does not that expression imply a place?

A. No; not so much a place as, an advance on the part of the spirit in purity; or, as the ancients taught, becoming so like unto God in holiness as to become gods. These ancients taught that the purer the life, the nearer to God; and they got such ideas from the spirit world. There is a great centre, the heaven of heavens—the throne of the great and holy spirit—whence flow out in copious streams His gracious influences to all, but especially to man, over all His vast and glorious kingdom.

Q. How do spirits control a medium?

A. In a hundred different ways. If I desired to have full and complete control of this medium, I would enter in. Having greater powers I would overrule him. He would, for the time being, be no longer himself. All his physical powers would be under my control. But the control I have is different; it is not possession. He is entranced by another, and I am at liberty to use him, and I do so in the same way as you would do were you prompting another individual to speak—with this difference; my medium has to translate into his own tongue that which I prompt him to say, and I, on the other hand, have to translate what you say as the sounds of your voice strikes on the spiritual atmosphere, in the way formerly described. It would be different, and much easier, were we acquainted with each other's language, or both speaking the same language. Again, when you sit at the table for manifestations, each one sitting emits a magnetism which envelopes you—a magnetic ring is formed, while the magnetism rises upwards like a cone or column; and when we come, our magnetism comes down and meets yours in the centre; having established this connection, we can operate on material things. Then we can use a medium's hand to write, by bringing our magnetism to bear on his arm from the elbow downwards; and on those whom we cannot thus act, we impress their brain, and they are made to write even while thinking of something else.

Q. *Do mediums give communications purporting to be from certain spirits when such is not the case?*

A. If mediums are not under the control of a particular spirit-guide, he or she is liable to be used by spirits of a disorderly character. There are always plenty of these standing around, ready to act whenever the conditions afford them an opportunity. Were I such a spirit, how easy would it be for me to give you a long story about this, that, and the other thing! But of this you need not be afraid, so long as the medium is in the habit of meeting with faithful and true spirits. These will never deceive you. Ask them a question on a subject they are ignorant of, and they will confess their ignorance, making no pretence to know more than they do. I have seen certain spirits at your circles, professing to know all about persons present, when, in fact, they knew little or nothing about them; and oftentimes our Indian friends have been with difficulty restrained from using violent measures with these pretenders.

Q. Does an individual's creed on earth affect his happiness in the spirit world?

A. It matters not whether he be a Jew, Mahommedan, or Christian. When I think of these Mahommedans my old nature gets up. Yet, even amongst them, there are good and true men who, faithful to the precepts of their prophet, put multitudes of Christians to shame. If Christians would but look as much to Jesus as these men do to Mahomet, it would be better for them. I have known noble-hearted men also amongst the Brahmins of India— men who, though differing in creed from Jews or Christians, were morally superior, and therefore more likely than multitudes of these to get a higher position in spirit-life. These were men who did not wear a cloak of religion, to put on once a week, but who served him whom they looked on as their lord every day. No matter by what name he was known to them, if they looked upon Him whom they worshipped as God; they might do so through the medium of an uncouth figure or image, but it was God, their maker and preserver, they meant to worship. But better than, and beyond all faiths and creeds, is it to walk in the steps of Jesus, my prince, who was sent to reveal the father to mankind—sent that he might become the light of the world.

Q. Is it necessary that prayer should find an expression in words?

A. No; you must have thoughts before words. Why, you might stand in silence before the world and pour out your soul in prayer to God. On the other hand, you might give utterance to words in sound like that of a trumpet—a mere form of words without the expression of your heart's desires—but that is not prayer.

Q. Would it be right to follow the advice of Jesus literally in regard to non-resistance, in his saying: 'If he smite thee on the one cheek, turn to him the other also'?

A. That is a figurative expression, meaning, to him who would injure you, you must return good. Such figures of speech were very common in Persia, India, and among all eastern nations. Jesus might have done this, but where will you find a man to do it? No, verily; human nature as it is would never comply with the injunction. Man has no right to allow his life to be taken away, either by a wild animal or a wild man. You are not a God, you are a man. You do not hesitate to kill a wild animal in self-defence; and what is he who lifts his murderous hand to take away another's life but a wild man, who must be restrained with all the force you are capable of exerting in defence of yourself or others.

Q. Are the ten commandments, as given in the Book of Moses, of divine origin?

A. I know little about the laws promulgated by the great Hebrew lawgiver. I would look on some of them as proceeding from the inspiration of good and true spirits through mediumship of Moses; but there are others which, in my opinion, are but man-made. We had laws in Persia (indeed, every nation had), professing to come from the great source; but I looked on them only as dictated by holy and good spirits to the lawgivers—given to them and received by them as divine. Notice this, however, that, even though the work of holy spirits, the medium through which they communicated might have been unable to do justice to the truths sought to be imparted; and again, such spirits, notwithstanding their good character, might have been wrong. If I thought it was proper for me to tell you something which I believed to be right, something worth your acceptance, I would certainly do it, and yet it might turn out to be wrong. Moses was evidently well acquainted with the hieroglyphic records of Egypt, and should have known that these place creation much further back than the time given in his account. There was something inconsistent in his character; for, besides this, notice how he himself trampled on one of the best of his laws—that which forbade the killing of a human being—by commanding the slaughter of the very people he was appointed to govern and protect. But it is not for me to criticise; faults may be found in the characters and lives of all good men in all nations.

Q. *A belief prevails among all Christian communities, founded on a statement of Jesus, that there is to be a great day of judgment, when the souls of all that ever lived must appear before Jesus, some for condemnation to a never-ending punishment, and some for the approval, and the enjoyment of everlasting happiness. Will you tell us what you know concerning this interesting subject?*

A. I know very little about the sayings ascribed to Jesus, during his ministry in Judea. Of one thing I am certain, and of which you also may be sure, that being an eastern and surrounded by easterns, he would frequently use figurative language to convey the truths which he desired to impart to his hearers. It may appear strange to you, but figurative language was easily understood by us. Indeed, an eastern can express his ideas much better by use of figures than without them. True, Jesus, the lord of heaven and earth, is the great judge. But the judgment-day is the day of death, when, as a spirit, you appear as it were before Him, from whom there is no hiding; for all is laid bare on entering the spirit world. According as your life has been in the body, so is the judgment—so is your place in the great world of spirits. There are some things appertaining to earth with which I have but recently become acquainted; indeed, I am picking up many things from our friend (the medium) connected with the life and teachings of Jesus during his three years' work—things of which I had no knowledge. When I inquire of him in regard to such matters, he gives me information in the way he has learned it; and then, communicating with Paul or Peter, I find that they throw quite a different light on the subject. It may appear strange to you that I should be so situated; but I am perplexed with the information I get through my medium in regard to the doctrines taught by the followers of Jesus at the present time; and vexed in spirit when I see his teachings so grossly perverted. There is a passage which the medium has brought to my notice regarding another saying of Jesus—that some of those standing by him should not see death till he should come again, and that his coming would be at the destruction of the world. Referring this point to Paul, he said it was true spiritually, but not literally. The statement referred to the great outpouring of the spirit at Pentecost, when there was an upheaving of long-cherished ideas—a moral convulsion—but not to the destruction of earth and all its works. No; that would throw the whole planetary system into confusion; nay, more, it would destroy it. And for what end? To wipe out of mortal existence the inhabitants of earth, which, contrasted with its sister worlds, is but pea to a very large pebble; to throw the whole of these glorious worlds into unutterable confusion—dashing them to pieces, in order that this small lobe may be put out of existence! No, no, no—it cannot be.

Q. Can you tell us anything about the constitution of the sun—is it a material body similar to our earth?

A. It is similar in construction, and governed by the laws which regulate your world. The earth and other planets with their satellites revolve round the sun; the sun again revolves round another great body and its satellites, and so on: suns and systems, all under the same great controlling law, which keeps all in beautiful order, revolve round the grand centre, the dwelling-place of the great and mighty spirit. He is the source of light, which is reflected from sun to sun, and from world to world, over all systems that float in the boundless ocean of space.

Q. Does any one of earth go immediately at death into the heavenly sphere?

A. When I speak of heaven I refer to the place and condition in which I exist now. If that is what you mean, then I say 'YES' to your question. But if you refer to the holy of holies, the central sun, the dwelling-place of the most high, spoken of in the Hebrew writings, then I say 'NO'. No one of mortal birth can enter therein, till he is purged of every taint of earthliness; not even the spirit of a child whose breath was stopped at birth, can enter immediately into that glorious place; for that innocent has, by its mortal birth, inherited certain earthly tendencies, and these, by a long course of education, must be rooted out, and the strength and virtue which are gained by a life of trials on earth must be acquired here by a slower process. Trials experienced in the body are much more advantageous in the education of man than the discipline of spirit-life. The longer man lives on earth the better; and if he has improved the opportunities of his long life wisely and well, he is blessed indeed.

Q. Have all spirits passed through the mortal body?

A. No; there are some—angels. If you choose to call them so—who are the messengers from the great and mighty one to us: these holy ones have never been joined to the mortal body, though all are in human form, even the highest and mightiest in creation—man is but modelled from them. Moses, in his account of man's creation, uses the following language—'Let us make man in our own image,' implying that the creator, the high and mighty God, consulted with these holy ones in regard to the work of man s creation.

Q. Was there a time when there was no outward manifestation of God—when nothing existed but God?

A. I do not know; but may I give you my opinion. I believe that the great father of all never existed alone; that wherever He is there you will find the manifestation of His power, His wisdom and His goodness in material existences. I do not see well how it could be otherwise. Nothing! What is nothing? If nothing but God existed at any time, then He was everything. The thin air you breathe, that is something material. The various gases are but the spirits of solid matter; they may be dispersed by the winds, but they are never lost; they again become matter, lying, as it were, in a dormant state, but they are not lost, for you have but to apply the proper means, and back to their spirit-life they go; and so it is throughout the boundless expanse of the universe.

Q. Do the lower animals exist in spirit?

A. They do. Wherever there is life there is spirit, and spirit never dies. The smallest speck, unseen by the naked eye, having life, is precious to the great creator: with or without brain or nerve, it is all the same. Take a microscope. Examine one of these tiny animals, and you will find in it the first and simplest developments of organic life, then go upwards in the scale of animal creation, step by step, as you ascend in your examination, you will see a uniform progress in development, till, coming to man, you will find combined in him all that you have seen in the animals below him. You will see a part of man in the beaver who builds a house, and in the little mole who tunnels for himself a road beneath the pathway of which you walk. These creatures, and a thousand more, you will find in man. There is nothing in him which you will not find in the creation around him — he is a world in himself.

Q. Is it possible for you to visit any of the worlds outside our planetary system?

A. Is it possible for me to visit any of the worlds outside our system? Well, we are certainly not bound to this, though, as with you on earth, we commonly look to the family here. We never leave except when sent by our great prince on embassies to another high prince of other worlds beyond. So great is the distance of some of these worlds, you might travel thousands of years before you would reach their battlements. It is now about two thousand years since I came here, and had I started then on such a mission, ten times two thousand years might be expended, and still I would be unable to reach the boundaries of creation. It is strange how short, apparently, is the space between the great central sun and us. Indeed, should we fly towards some distant planet, away, as it were, from the centre, we find on reaching our destination, that there is no perceptible difference — we seem to be as near to it as ever; so that each of the systems appears to be as near to the great central sun as another, although in reality some do, at times, get nearer than others. The inhabitants of the various planets differ somewhat, physically and intellectually. Some are mere babes when you are full grown men.

Q. Is it true as some philosophers have asserted, that the sun is a body of fire?

A. It is absurd to say so. The heat which you get from the sun does not come from a body of fire, but arises from the position which the earth occupies in relation to the sun. You do not get heat from the moon, and yet you have light therefrom. The earth absorbs the heat produced by the sun's rays, and not only absorbs, but, according to the season of the year, throws off the heat. Take a crystal, and place it at a certain focus, and you absorb the heat; but put it out of focus, and you lose the heat. The nearer you approach the sun, you have the less heat. According to the position of the earth and other bodies in relation to the sun, so is the heat.

Q. How is it with mercury? There, it i said, the heat must be unbearable.

A. He is smaller, and the heat is just according to the focus of rays. Do you suppose God made these worlds merely to please His fancy, unfit for life? No, no; every one of them has its inhabitants, and these are, in general, purer and better than those on earth. Their state of creation is of course governed by the conditions of the planet in question—their material structure not being at all like your own, by that I mean *your* eyes might not be capable of seeing them, but they exist nonetheless.

Q. Have you spiritual food with which you are sustained?

A. Yes. Yet we could eat your food and drink your water; but before we could absorb them they would have to be spiritualised.

Q. You have said that you might spend twenty thousand years in flight towards the boundaries of creation, and be unable to reach them. Is it the same with the great ones, the messengers of the most high?

A. No; though the same in form, they are far superior to us in power, never having been in connection with the material body. I have some difficulty in getting you to comprehend this, there being nothing in all creation to which I may liken the quickness of their flight. It is quicker than thought, if you can conceive of such. The difference is very great between their flight and ours, quick as that is. No gross material form has left its heavy impress upon these holy ones; but, coming direct from the creative hand of the great maker, they are pure. No doubt we are the offspring of the same great father, but we came in a different way. These holy ones are not only pure, sinless, but as God himself, making the lightnings of heaven their chariots.

Q. *Can there be bounds to creation?*

A. I cannot tell, as I have said before, though we should live throughout eternity, we shall never be able to find out the extent of God's work.

Q. *Am I right in concluding, from all you have been saying to us, that we can never form any idea of the person of the most high, and that the only God that can be personally manifested to us is the anointed one—Jesus the prince?*

A. He is the only representation which mankind in the body can have of God. But I am more and more inclined to believe that the great and mighty spirit, the master of all worlds, the father of us all, is in the likeness of man. The intelligent beings of every world are similar in shape and form, and therefore I conclude that the great father, in bringing forth his children, formed them in his own likeness—that, in sending His son into the world, he sent him in his own image.

Q. Do the great rulers of the other worlds—those whom you refer to as the 'anointed ones,' and as being like Jesus the prince—ever visit you?

A. O yes; and they are like him. But high and holy, beyond all description, though they be, Jesus the prince stands higher, and is greater than they. And why? Because he has trod the earth in material body, and has thus been subjected to trials which they have never experienced—thereby accomplishing more than any other. In the eyes of the holy ones he is nearer to the great father than any one, and is so held in the estimation of all his subjects.

Q. Do you know of any other material world, the inhabitants of which are in the same condition morally as those of the earth?

A. No; they seem never to have risen in pride against the laws of the creator.

Q. On one occasion you spoke of a material world that had been destroyed because of the wickedness of the inhabitants.

A. Yes, I did. I had no knowledge of it from my own experience, but I have heard it referred to by others in the great temple. In that case there was no deliverer. That world was totally destroyed, but not the spirits of its inhabitants. Their bodies were swept away, but they themselves have long since been raised to holiness and glory. I have known of worlds—what you would call worlds—that have been broken up; but these were worlds in process of formation—I mean comets. These, as I have already said, are composed, in their first condition, of gases, and these gases, getting on fire, the vast mass rushes off in its course, blazing though space, and at length, after millions of years, it begins to cool on its external surface; a crust is formed, and the nearest system of planets draws the new world within the circle of its influence, when it moves on in regular procession.

Q. Are those high and holy, ones, who are the rulers of systems of worlds, the creators of worlds?

A. I do not know. But it seems to me that all creation is but the effect of laws laid down by *the* great spirit. Creation is ever going on.

Q. It is said in one of the gospels, referring to Him who is there called 'the word'— 'All things are made by him, and without him was not anything made.'

A. Moses, in his account of creation, says; 'Let us make man in our own image.' Who are the *us* who were thus called to take part in creation? I believe it refers to our prince and the others. The great and mighty spirit, as it were, called them into His counsels in the great work; though, so far as Moses was concerned, he gives merely what tradition had imparted to him—not revelation.

Q. In the instruction of the children in the spirit world, do any of them imbibe evil ideas whereby they might be led into sin, and so fall into a lower sphere or condition?

A. No; they know nothing of earth's evils. When they come here they are placed under the guardianship of teachers whose instructions never fail in leading the spirits under their care to the love of wisdom and goodness. But, when these come to mature spirit-life—to manhood, so to speak, they look down upon us on earth, and have often much cause to grieve when they perceive the prevailing evils of mankind.

Q. What sort of musical instruments were in use in the east in your day?

A. We had what you call a drum, low and narrow, and beaten on one end; then there was a pipe with holes, blown upon by the mouth; the flute; we had silver horns, having a great many twists, with an open mouth; several stringed instruments, some made of metal, which were struck with soft hammers; and we had also bells of varied tones and strength, set in frames.

Q. When you were on earth how did you measure time?

A. By the sun generally: I mean, by sun-dials We also used the sand-glass for the same purpose.

Q. There are large numbers of Christians who pray to Mary as the 'mother of God.' What is your opinion of the matter?

A. The mother of God! They may be what you call Christians, but certainly they are not the followers of Jesus. Mary was, indeed, a very blessed woman, but she could never be the mother of God.

Q. Did you ever meet any ancient Britons?

A. Yes; I met with them in Greece and Rome. Some of them were Christians. There was a good deal of intercourse kept up by the Romans, and by the ships which took out the produce of the east to these western islands in exchange for tin ore.

Q. Is suicide under extreme physical pain justifiable?

A. No, it is not justifiable. The man who takes away that which belongs to another is a thief. Man's life is the gift of God; and if he, unbidden, cuts that life short, he robs God. Punished he will be; there is no escape. A long, dreary, and wretched time awaits him in those dark regions already spoken of, before he is brought, by the fires of conscience, to see his error and get free.

Q. *Can spirits who have lived on other planets of the solar system visit the earth and communicate as you do with mortals?*

A. No, you on earth are unlike the beings who dwell on the other planets, You are much more materialised—not so spiritual in your nature. You have more of the animal, and less of the divine. The beings who inhabit the other worlds are purer, more spiritual, not so gross in body as those of earth—so much so that we can converse freely with them, while they can see and hear us, and can handle us when we come near to them. Clothed as you are, therefore, with the earth-body, the spirits of the other worlds cannot come into contact with you as we do who are of the earth; but when you come into the sprit world they will be able to associate with you, if you are in a state similar to them.

Q. *Is the original cause of evil to be traced to the thing called 'Satan'?*

A. Where do you get your information about such a being? You will hardly find it in the Hebrew records; if there, the writers must have borrowed the idea from the Persians and Chaldeans. At one time, when on earth, I believed firmly in the existence of such a being; but I discarded the doctrine. In the Persian or Zoroastrian system, there was a god of evil, not unlike the one spoken of by Jewish writers. We now know that there is no such a potentate. Man alone in the originator of evil. He fell

169

away from his happy, innocent state by pride, and became what he is now, and ever will be, until the race becomes what it was before child-like, and open to higher and holier influences.

Q. Our Bible speaks of Jesus being tempted by the devil—offered the whole world if he will but fall down and worship him.

A. This is clearly the original writer's way of expressing that Jesus was tempted by *men* to forsake the work he had been sent to do. It is one more example of the way eastern peoples tell stories to illustrate the idea they wish to give the listener or reader; you western people take everything too literally; clearly this is why you have so misunderstood much that is in your Gospels; not just you the people, but those priests among you who should know better.

Q. Were the many places in Persia in a waste or desert condition when you were on the earth?

A. There were a few places waste, not many, in my day. These were caused by the inroads of the Romans and others, when the people fled, leaving the land to be pillaged and to become waste. Before my day, all except the most mountainous parts were under cultivation.

Q. Paul says of Jesus, 'He thought it not robbery to be equal with God.' Does not Paul here contradict what you have often asserted—that Jesus is not the deity?

A. I still assert the same, and Paul does not contradict me. Jesus stood in the place of the city Himself, to speak of a rebellious world. What medium in heaven or on earth could bring back the spirit which had broken the link that bound him to the body? Not all the spirits in heaven combined could restore me to the body. The chain—the silver cord—once snapped, can no more be joined. Jesus my prince, and he alone, could do it; for on him was bestowed all power of the great spirit, and from him only could the power proceed. Have I not seen him, in the fullness of that power, order the spirit back to the body? In the fullness of that power he rules in heaven, earth, and hell—the great governor over all this system of worlds. Paul does not contradict my assertions; for, you will notice, he does not say, 'He *was* equal with God,' but that 'he thought it not *robbery* to be equal with God,' inasmuch as the divine power he wielded was the *gift* of Him who alone could bestow it. There was no robbery—there could be none—for to Jesus was given the spirit without measure. He was the very embodiment of the great spirit; yet he himself never said, 'I am the great spirit, the source of all being the creator and father of all.'

Q. But John, in the Gospel ascribed to him, says, 'All things were made by him—'

A. Had I not had many opportunities of studying Jesus, I might have come to a different conclusion on this point. Many times I could have worshipped him, and had I been Greek instead of Persian, this would have been the case; but, conversant with the prophecies about him, I was prepared to receive him as indeed he was—the great deliverer sent by God. How his disciples should come to entertain any other idea, I do not know.

Q. You said that you found the Hebrew account of the plagues verified by inscriptions on ancient Egyptian tablets But Hermes says he can find no trace of such. Will you explain?

A. Well, I could read hieroglyphics, he could not, at least not so well. And then he is an Egyptian, and not disposed to admit the fact. But the hieroglyphic records are hardly so forcible in the description as those of the Hebrew writer.

Q. *What does the name Zoroaster signify?*

A. The name in the ancient Persian signifies one who gives himself entirely to divine influence, one who secludes himself from the world. But, though he shut himself up in a cave, the great reformer was not unmindful of his brethren of mankind; for he sacrificed much to benefit his fellow-men.

Q. *Did he live long before the time of Moses?*

A. According to our records, he did not live long before the great Hebrew. It might be about one hundred years.

Q. *Can you tell me anything about the second advent of Christ?*

A. I have already spoken on that subject. I have told you he will never appear on the earth again in the body of flesh—here, and now, he appears as our great prince, the sovereign ruler of the worlds of our system. Not again will he become a child of earth, from which he was violently cast forth by cruel men—a martyr for the truth. But, though now ascended to his kingdom, he has still the same love for men—he still compassionates that world which murdered him, and he still visits you in spirit. When his second advent is spoken of in your sacred books, it refers to the grand time in your world's future history, when mankind shall be so spiritual, so holy in life, that we who have passed away from earth will be able to commune face to face with mortal man, and also influence him for good to a far greater extent than we can now. Then indeed, shall he come—then, truly, shall he walk the earth—when his sway shall extend from sea to sea, reigning by his truth and love in the hearts of men.

Q. Is that time near at hand?

A. Alas! No. There are mighty barriers in the way, that must be removed before such a spirit communion as I have spoken of be at all possible. The evils that find a lodgment in the hearts of men must be expelled. Men must become believers in the great spirit, and thorough spiritualists; there must be no cowardly hiding the truth—no longer the fear of the world; but with open hearts and unstammering tongues, men must proclaim the truth within them; the unholy alliance of evil and good must be denounced; in fact, the precepts of Jesus must be practically carried out before the glorious time come on, so long and so anxiously desired by holy men of all ages. Then shall man be open to the good and holy influences of the spirit world, and the golden age return never more to pass away. Earth will be no longer a scene of suffering, but a school for the better life on high, even the entrance door to heaven.

Questions Answered

by

HERMES

Q. Do you suppose the pyramids to have been built prior to the deluge recorded by Moses?

A. I can find no trace in Egyptian records of such a deluge at the date given by Moses. How he got everything so definite—so clearly stated in reference to it, is altogether beyond my comprehension, for I can trace the facts of history far beyond that ascribed to the deluge. The Egyptian records place the deluge much farther back. But Moses was just the man to adapt such stories to suit his purpose. I believe he begins his account from the time when mankind were in an innocent condition—when the Egyptians were a happy race of shepherds—that golden age when the spirit world held communion with mortals; it was then, according to his account, that evil crept in, and mankind was bitten by the serpent, the symbol of wisdom and of power, because of the fascination lodged in his beautiful eyes. I have no doubt whatever that the earliest of these pyramids was erected long before the date assigned to the deluge recorded by Moses.

Q. What is your opinion of the doctrine of reincarnation?

A. I believe in incarnation. Man, spiritually, being the offspring of God, is, as I have said, something infinite in nature. In his prior existence, he shuffles off the spirit body he received from God, and takes on the carnal—he becomes incarnated. But putting off the mortal, he never returns to the material state. Why, that would be a new creation!

Q. How is it that such a doctrine is taught by spirits?

A. I will tell you how. Had I left the body while I was simply an Egyptian priest, I would have tried (had I been communicating) to explain such subjects according to the ideas I then entertained, and would have continued to do so, until my eyes were opened by superior light. You must not take everything as correct merely because it comes from spirit. You must judge of that which is communicated. If it commends itself to reason, accept it; if not, reject it.

Q. *I should like to have an account from you of the personal appearance of Jesus.*

A. Well, I knew him when he was a little boy in Egypt. But when I met him in Judea, I was startled; for, as I looked on him, he appeared to me more than man: there was something in his face that told me plainly I was in the presence of no mere mortal. His countenance beamed with a light not natural. When he spoke, his voice went into the very depths of my soul. In bodily appearance, he was rather tall; slender, but yet proportionate. There was somewhat of the Roman in his cast of countenance. His hair was a fairish auburn, parted in the middle of his head, and hanging over his shoulders. His eyes were black, sharp, and piercing, with a depth of expression not mortal.

Q. *Did his disciples understand the relation you bore to him?*

A. Yes; he had told them that he knew me in Egypt, and that we were both educated by the same tutor—the venerable Issha. I have often wondered why all notice of his education in Egypt has been left out of the narratives of his mission handed down to you; for I remember that one of his disciples, Matthew, had just before we were scattered by persecution, written a narrative of the work, and he had heard what Jesus had said on the matter. At that time I was just about being sent away on a mission to the land of my birth.

Q. Were there amongst the twelve disciples the brothers of Jesus, the sons of Joseph and Mary?

A. No; but there were brothers of Jesus amongst the other disciples. He chose the twelve outside his own family, although both James and John were very nearly related to him; and they had been his bosom companions when at home, from the time when he came back the second time from Persia. Indeed, the love of John and Jesus was very remarkable: where you found the one, it was said, you might be sure to find the other. When the little band sat down to rest or to eat, John always sat on the right hand of the master. He was the last of the twelve who left the earth—living, I believe, to a very advanced age, just as if to shown how a quiet, loving spirit could be held in the midst of troubles and grievous persecution.

Q. Do all spirits know the future?

A. No; but in some cases, under certain conditions, they can tell what is about to happen; but this knowledge is not their own. If they are interested in the welfare of a person, one under their care, they may receive knowledge of the future in regard to their charge from a higher source. The guardian spirit may be unable to prevent that which is foreseen—say a shipwreck; but he may impress on his charge in such a way as to cause him, when bent on going with the ship, to miss his passage. The vessel sails without him. He hears of the disaster which befalls her, and cries out, 'O, how lucky it was I was unable to get with her!' There was no luck in it. It was pure prevention by his guardian spirit.

Q. Can you inform me if any of the natives of Britain were disciples of Jesus?

A. There were some of your countrymen serving as Roman soldiers in Judea, who became followers of the master, and these, when they returned to their own country, proclaimed the truth they had received. There had been a long time intercourse kept up by the Tyrian trade in tin.

Q. *Was the company at what is called the last supper confined to the twelve?*

A. No; but it was confined to the disciples who were with the master at the time, including the twelve. In this he made no distinction; he looked on all as his brethren. We were all dear to Jesus, but these twelve, being Hebrews, he chose to be his body servants.

Q. *You say Jesus was taken from the high priest to Herod, and then to Pilate. In one of the four Gospels the writer says he was taken from the high priest's to Pilate, who remitted him to Herod, and that the latter sent him back to Pilate. Is there no mistake in your statement?*

A. No; my statement is correct.

Q. *Did you eat and drink with Jesus after the resurrection?*

A. On several occasions he ate and drank with the assembled brethren.

Q. *Was there not something different in his bodily powers—something greater than before his crucifixion?*

A. No; there was then no greater power. He did not at all times put forth his power. On some occasions, during his ministry in Judea, he disappeared from the sight of his enemies: in these cases he merely operated on their eyesight. By the exercise of the same power after his resurrection he appeared to us and vanished away. Had our beloved master wished to escape at Calvary, do you imagine that nails could have held him to the cross? No. And there were those about him who, had he but said the word, could, in an instant, have swept his murderers from the face of the earth. But the cross was his final sermon; for on it he showed to all men that truth and righteousness must be maintained by the sacrifice of life itself if need be. On that dark day nature herself preached to many men of thought. Some tried to get over it by saying it was an eclipse of the sun; but wiser men knew that that could not take place at that time.

By the same author:

HAFED a Prince of Persia

'One of Spiritualism's greatest classics'
'One of the most beautiful writings ever received from spirit' ... ' A wonderful book'

(Greater World)

'Out of print for many years this edition is well worth acquiring. Absorbing reading'

(Psychic News)

'Difficult to do it justice in a review'
(Unitarian Society for Psychical Studies)

REVIEWS OF ORIGINAL BOOK (1876)

'It has an interest for us greater than the contents of any other book outside the Holy Scriptures - All Christian ministers should make themselves acquainted with this book'
(Glasgow Christian News)

'Of the greatest importance - One of the most extraordinary works that has appeared in connection with Spiritualism'
(The Spiritual Magazine, London)

'Viewed simply as a work of imagination, literature has nothing to equal this marvellous narrative'
(Religio Philosophical Journal, Chicago, USA)

Paperback £4.95

JESUS the WHOLE story

What **DID** God Say?

FLESH - the great illusion (Autobiography)

'Fascinating'   (Derek Jameson)

'Extremely interesting'   (Ned Sherrin)

'Could not put it down until I had read it from cover to cover'
                                                 (Ray Parkes)

'He writes with a conversational directness which means any messages the book might have are unintentional'
                                                 (Gay Times)

'An earthy caring person with psychic awareness and spiritual understanding'
                                                 (Scene Out)

'An extremely honest and graphic account of his life, this autobiography from spiritual healer, Ronal Wright is far removed from the usual approach adopted by such practitioners. "FLESH" is certainly no safe and cosy Spiritualist autobiography. Even in these so-called enlightened times it is still a brave book. Many may find it totally shocking, others unpleasant or distasteful. But whatever ones reaction Ronald has to be admired for his almost too blatant honesty.
This book is disarmingly candid and where, relevant, exceedingly sexually explicit. Were it not written with such naturalness and refreshing candour, some might argue that it ran the risk of bordering on the pornographic, but because it is presented in such an amiable and open manner, "FLESH" does not fall into the trap of being outrageous simply for the sake of it. An honest account from an honest man, this certainly makes controversial reading.'
                                                 (Psychic News)

Paperback £8.65   Hardback £14.95